My Toddler 1st
LEARNING BOOK

ABCs, 123s
&
other fun
ACTIVITIES

A note from the author:

As a mother of 3 beautiful kids, I designed this book to present parents and caregivers' different ways to teach your child to love learning. Bursting with exciting challenges, the ABCs, 123s and other fun toddler coloring book makes it tons of fun for your young scholar to develop the skills and abilities necessary to begin their scholastic journey.

Using kids coloring books is a great way to start learning. Using their hand to draw is a first step in learning handwriting. Using crayons as opposed to typing on a computer, fires up specific areas of a child's brain, improving their ability to not only remember what he or she
learns but to think of new ideas.

This is more than just a coloring book, kids can also learn numbers, basic math, and following directions. Activities appear in order of increasing difficulty, so preschoolers stay challenged until the end, constantly expanding their skills through reinforcement learning. With the funny and kid friendly illustrations and easy directions and visual clues, this
preschool workbook is fun and easy to use.

When kids finish the workbook, you can fill out the included "Great Job! You're #1" completion certificate to reward a job well done.

Letters

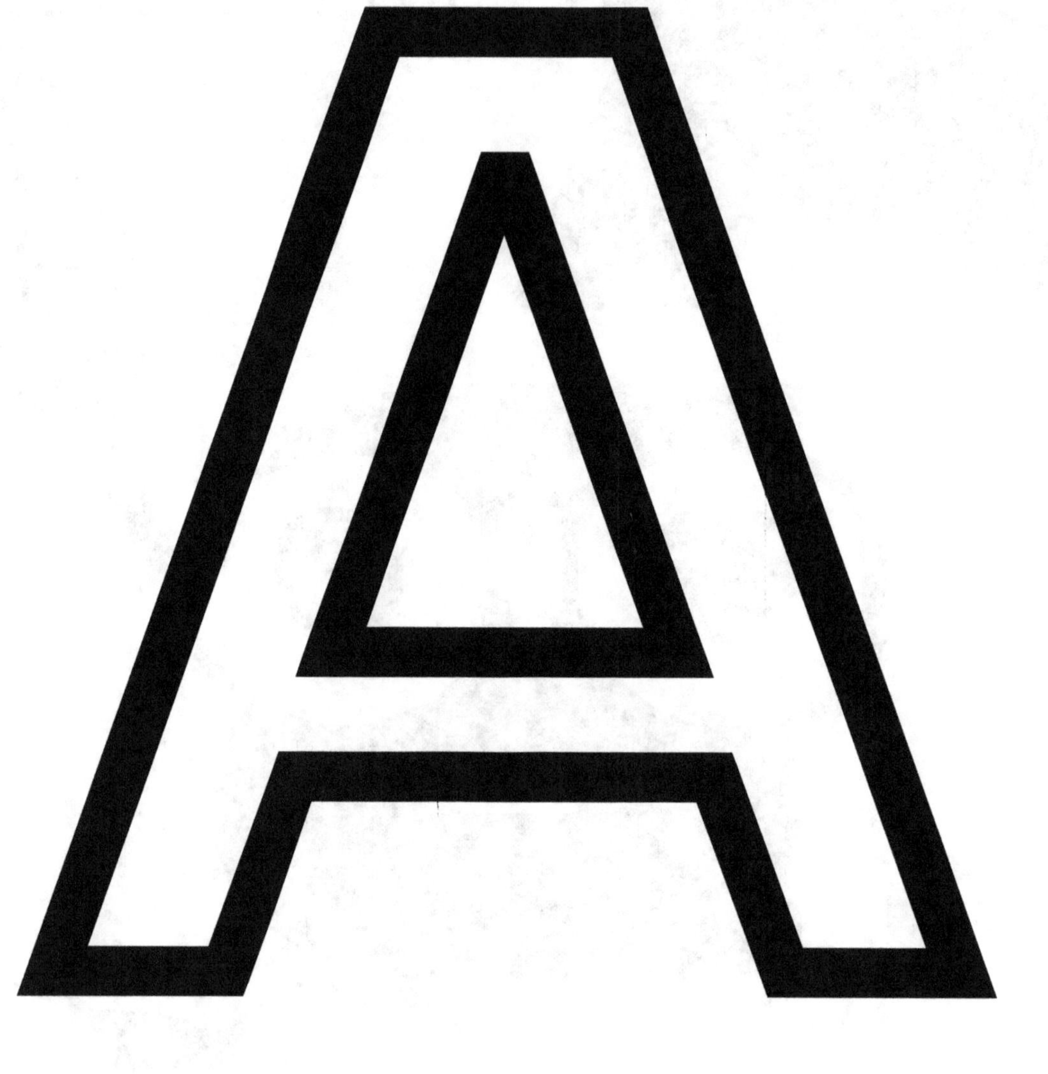

A

Color only the squares with letter A

B

B

Color only the squares with letter B

Color only the squares with letter C

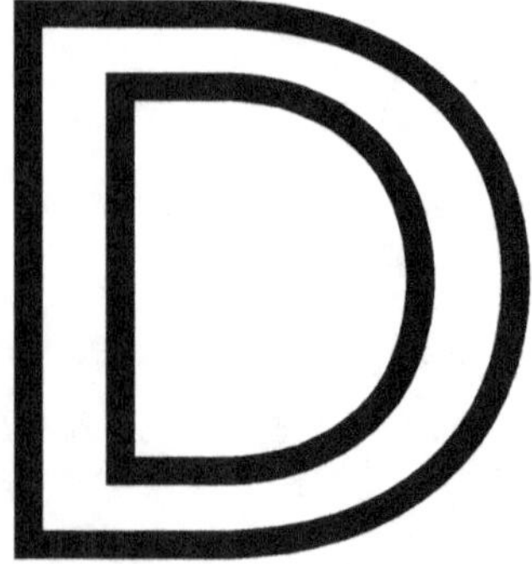

D

Color only the squares with letter D

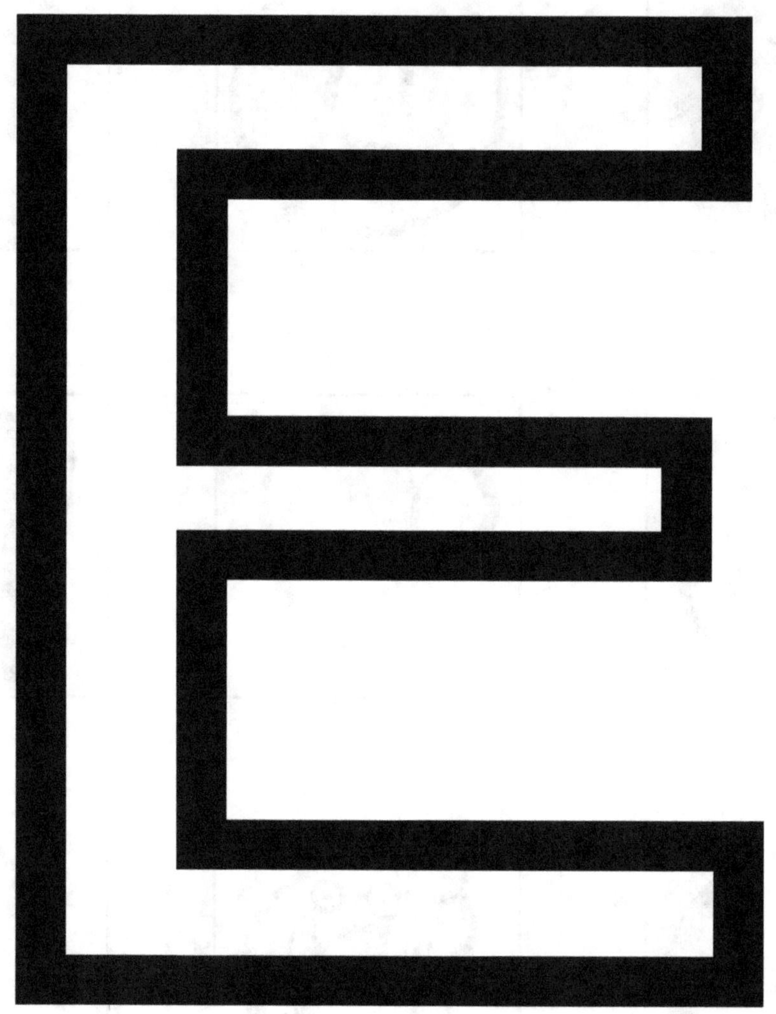

E

Color only the squares with letter E

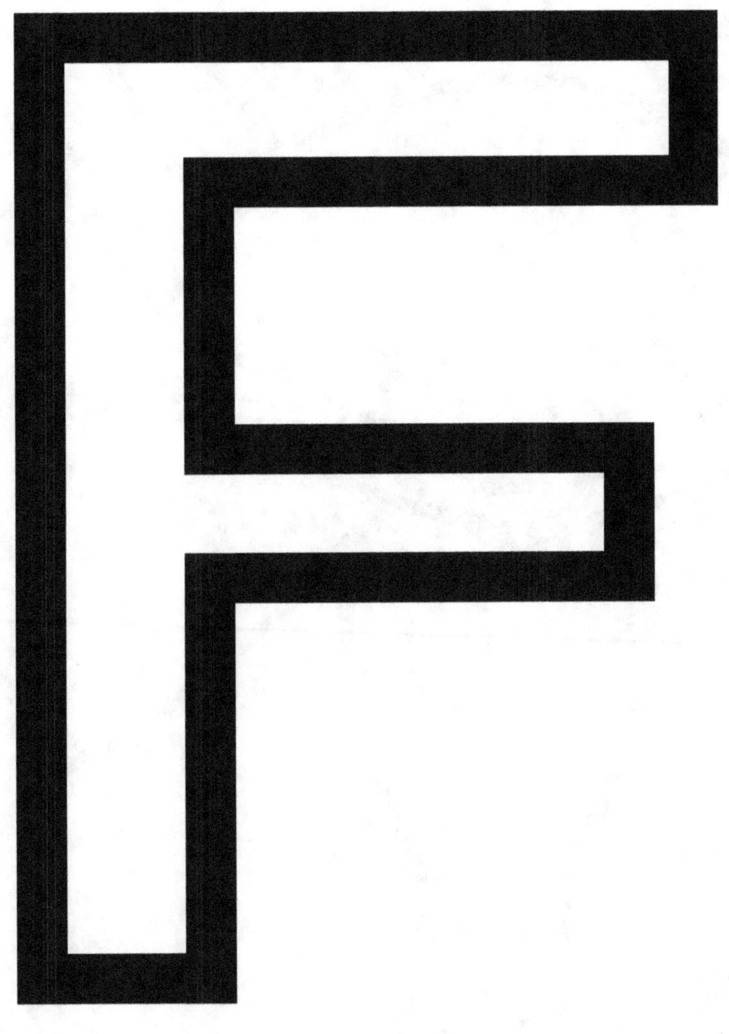

F

Color only the squares with letter F

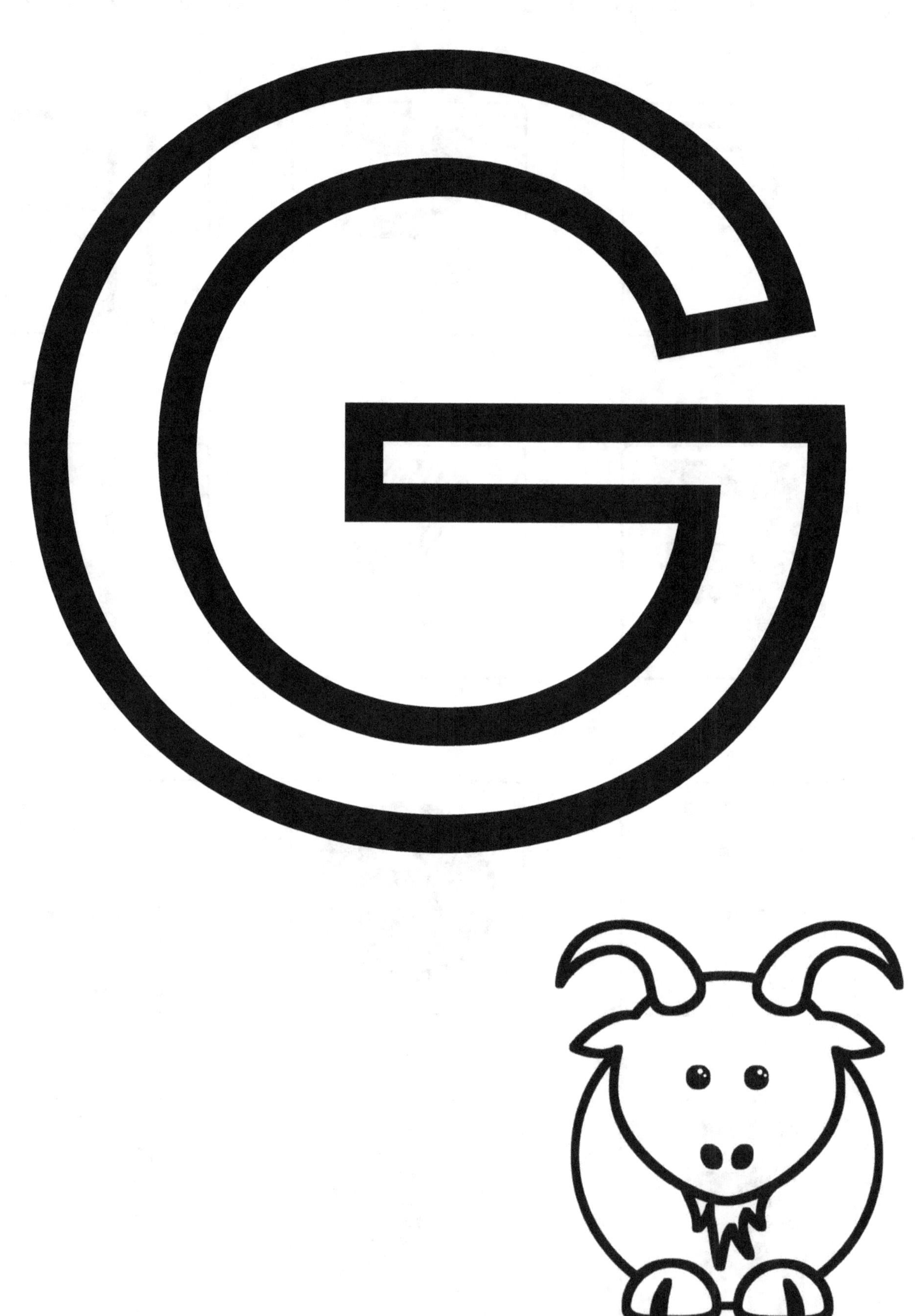

G

Color only the squares with letter G

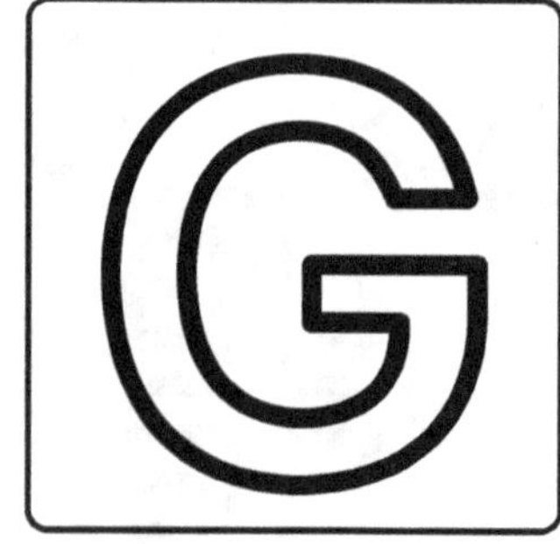

H

H

Color only the squares with letter H

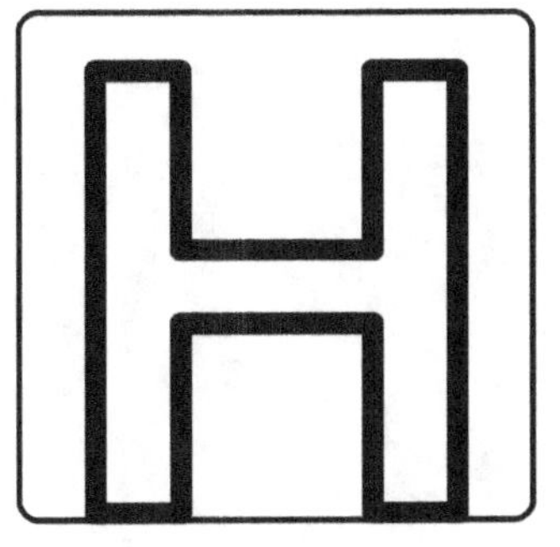  
  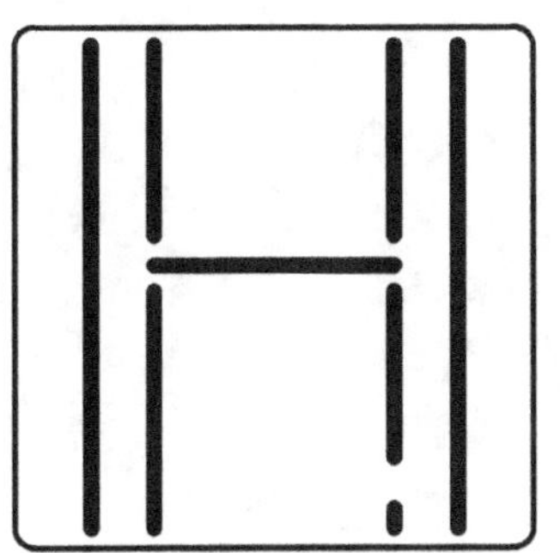

Color only the squares with letter I

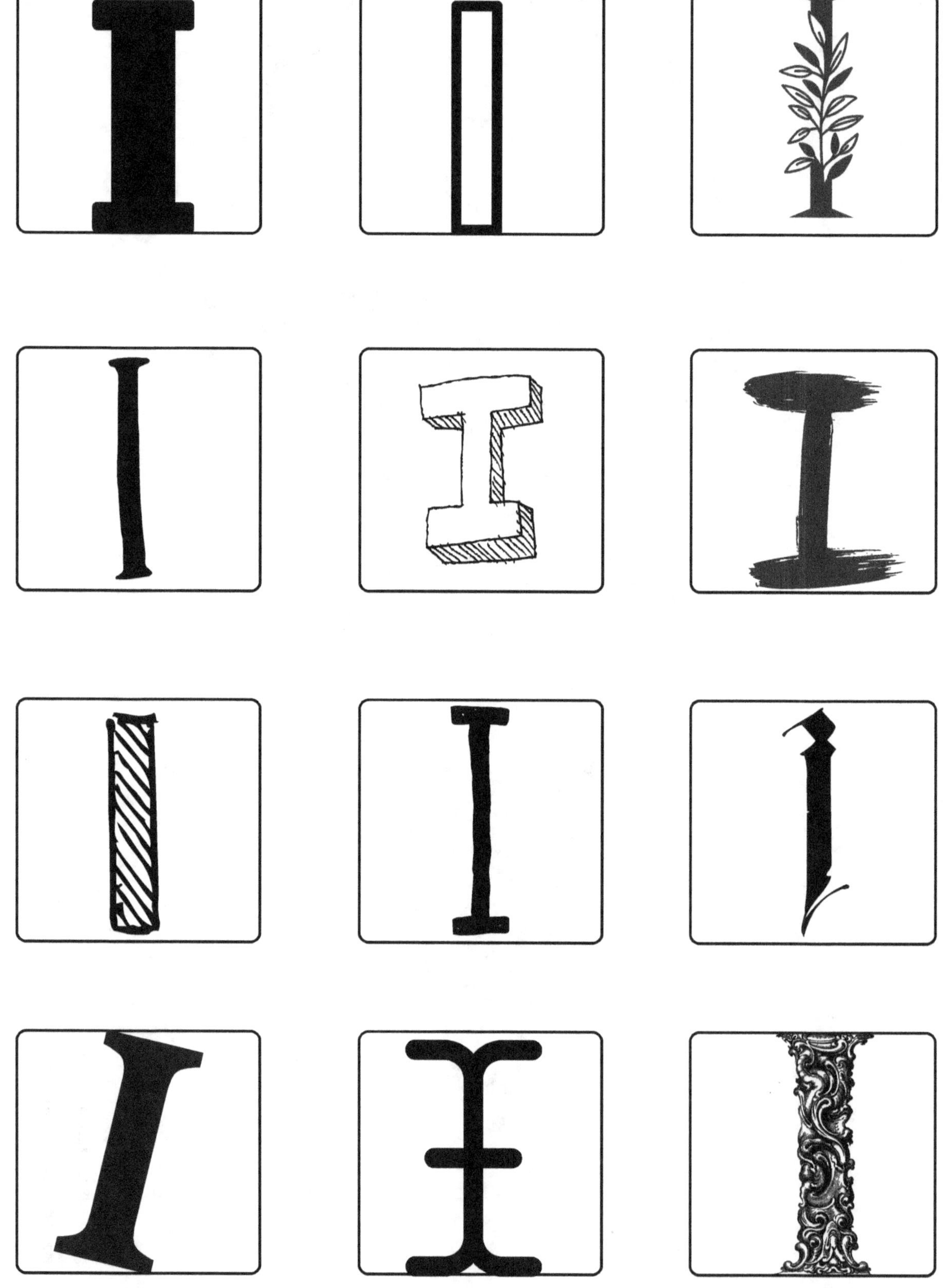

J

J

Color only the squares with letter J

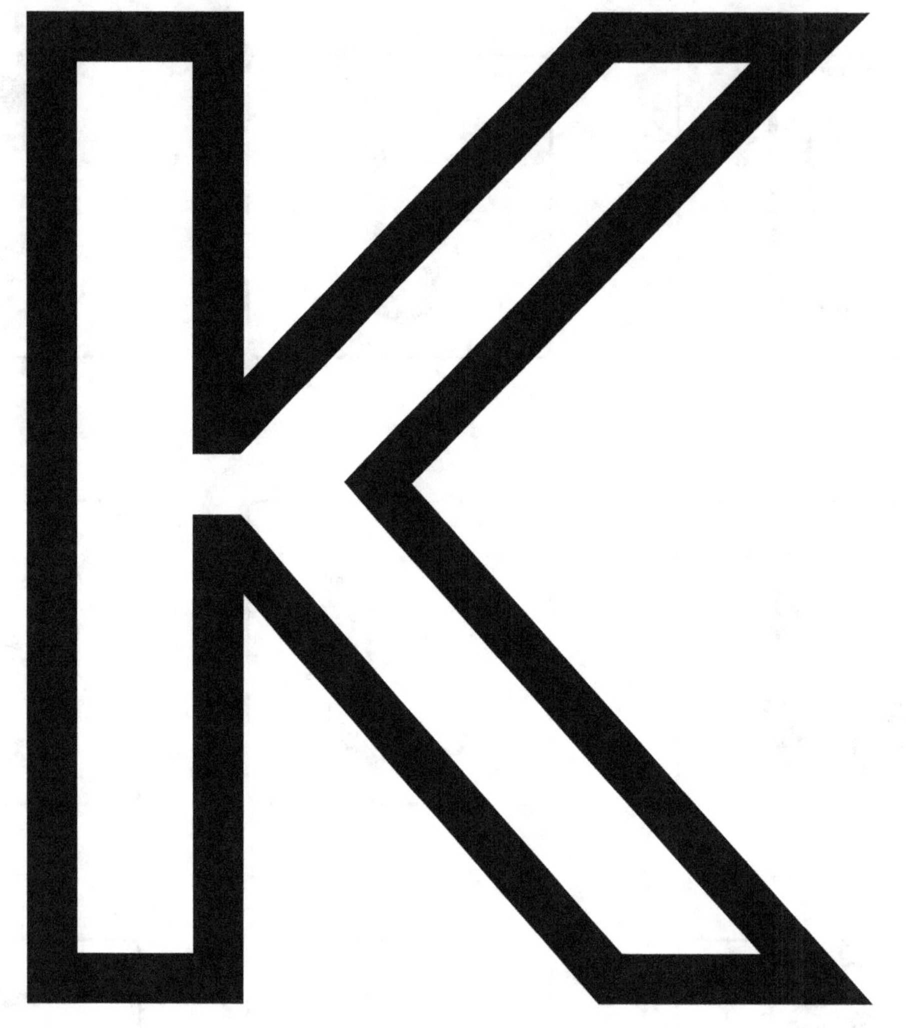

K

Color only the squares with letter K

L

Color only the squares with letter L

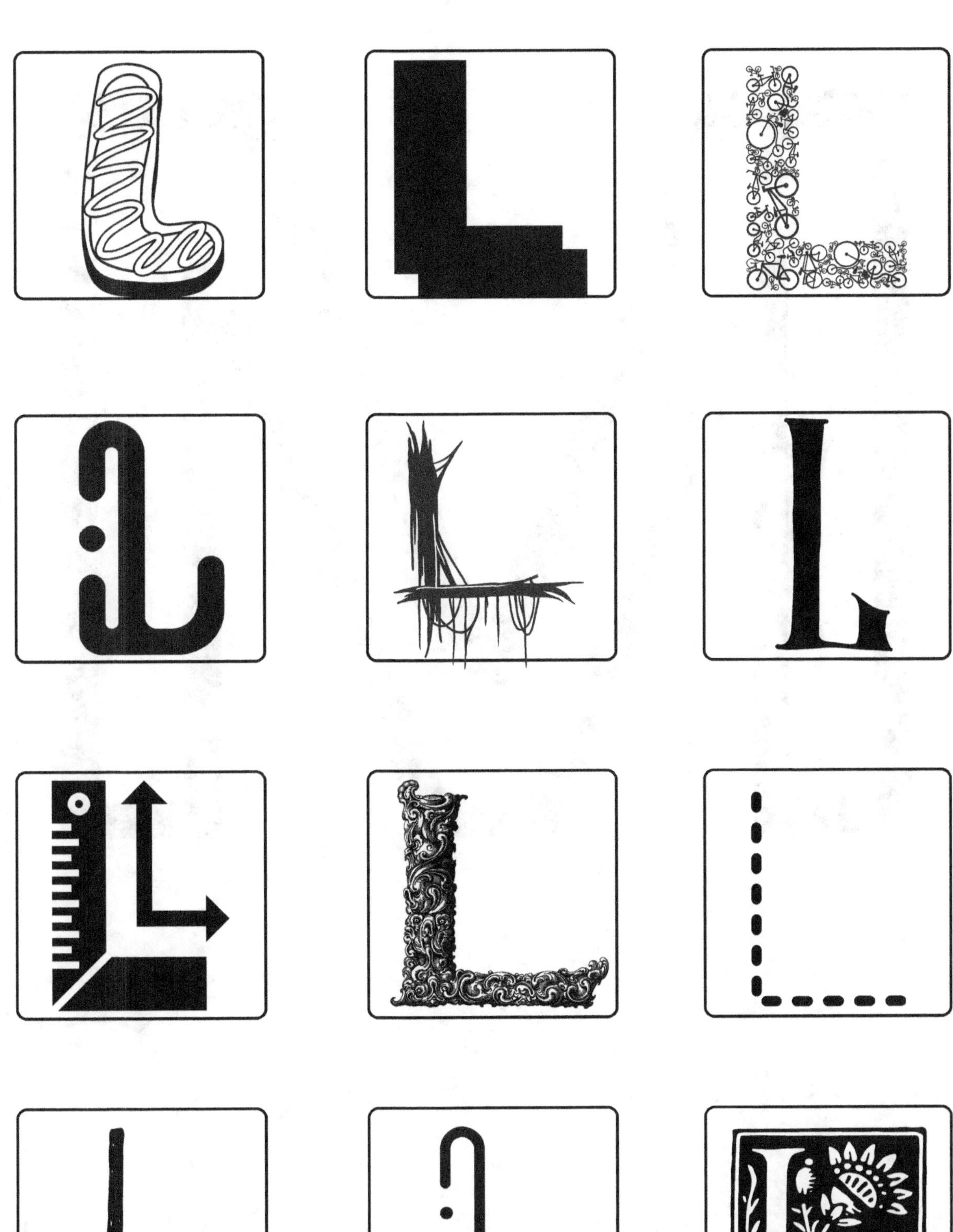

M

M

Color only the squares with letter M

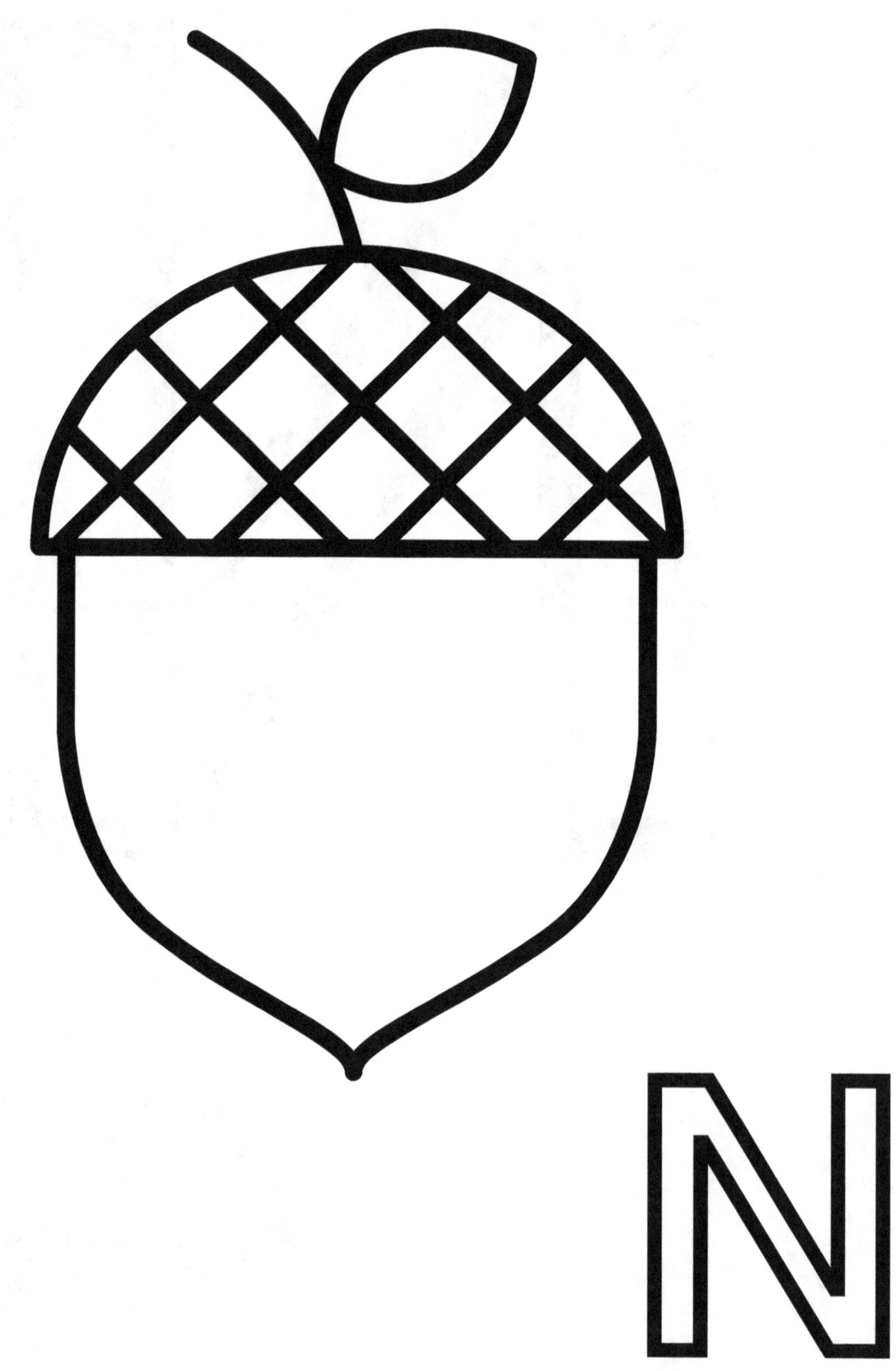

N

Color only the squares with letter N

  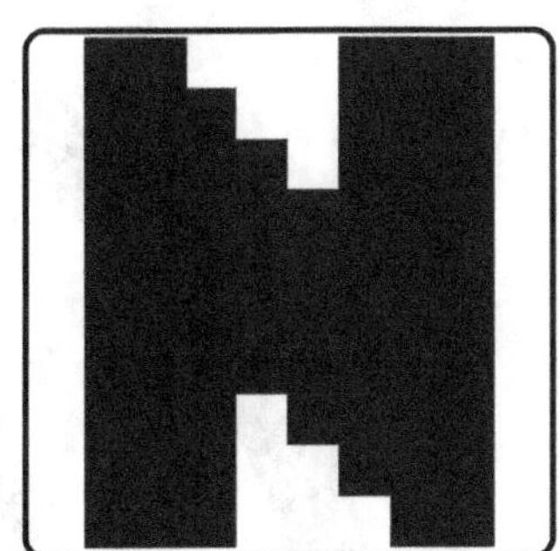

  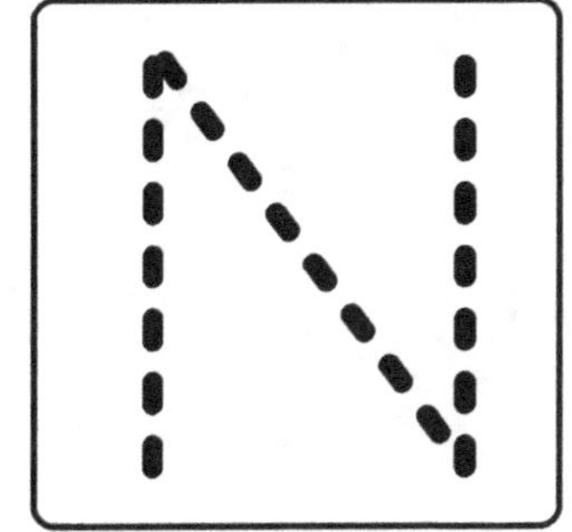

Color only the squares with letter O

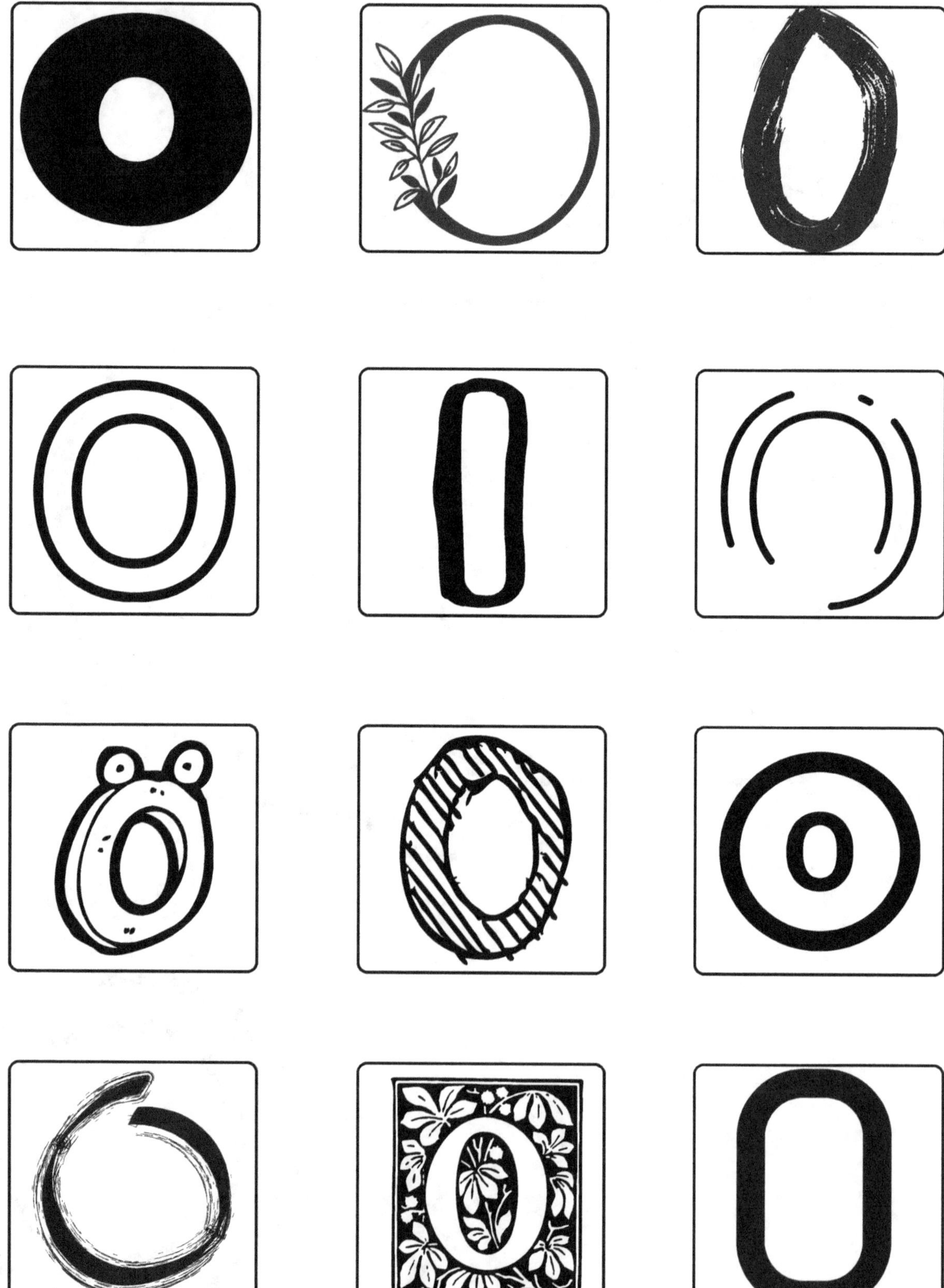

P

P

Color only the squares with letter P

Color only the squares with letter Q

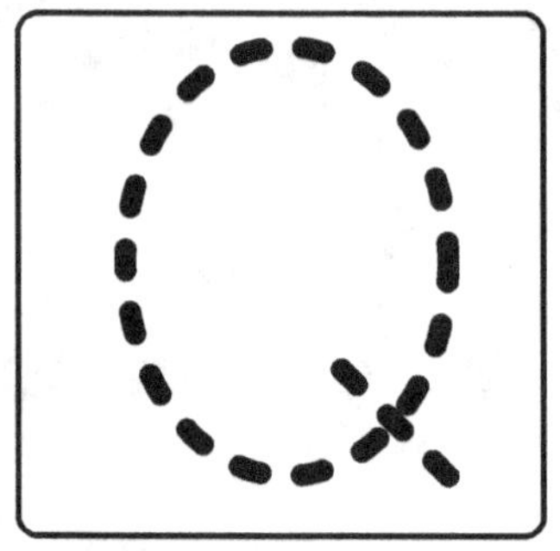  

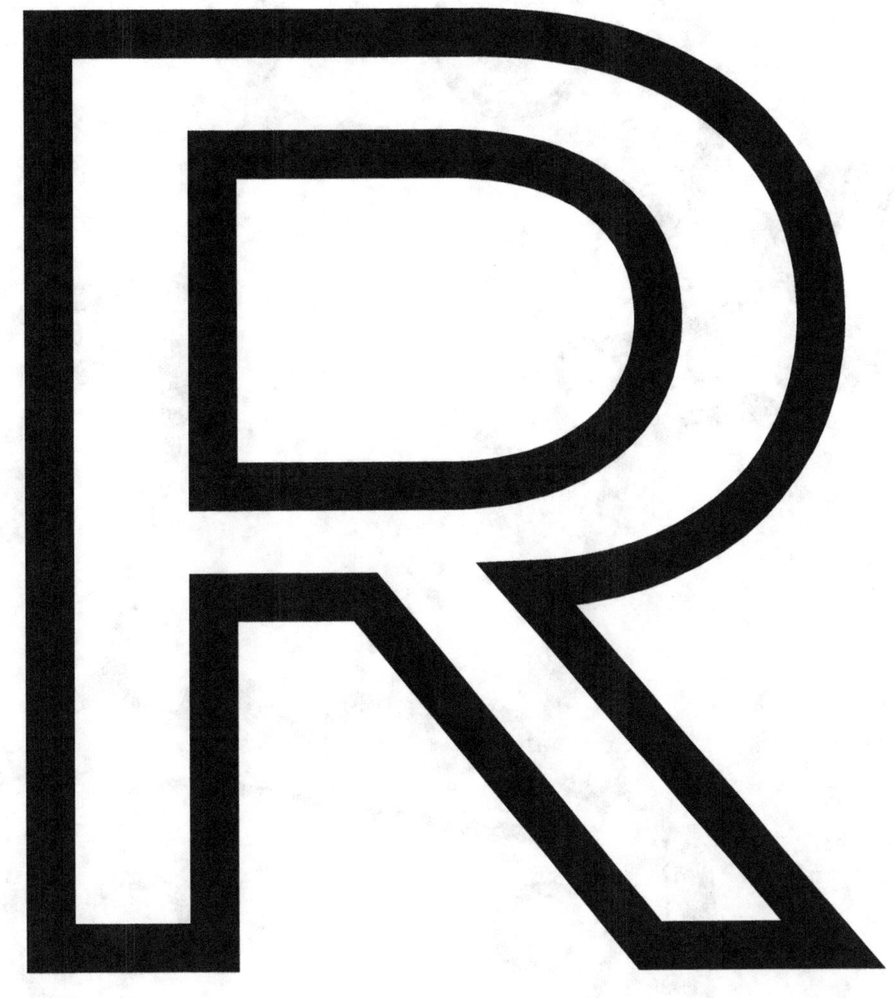

R

Color only the squares with letter R

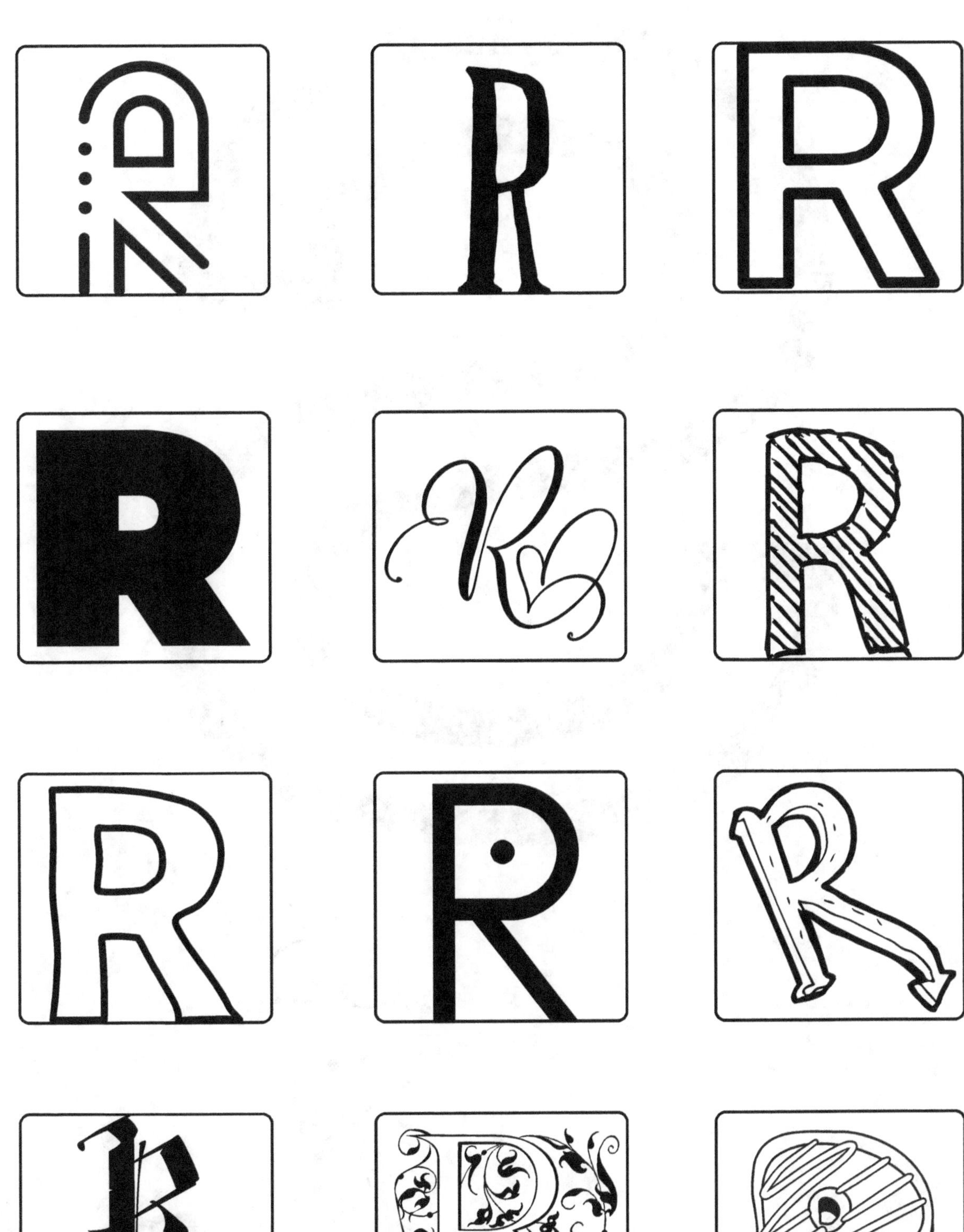

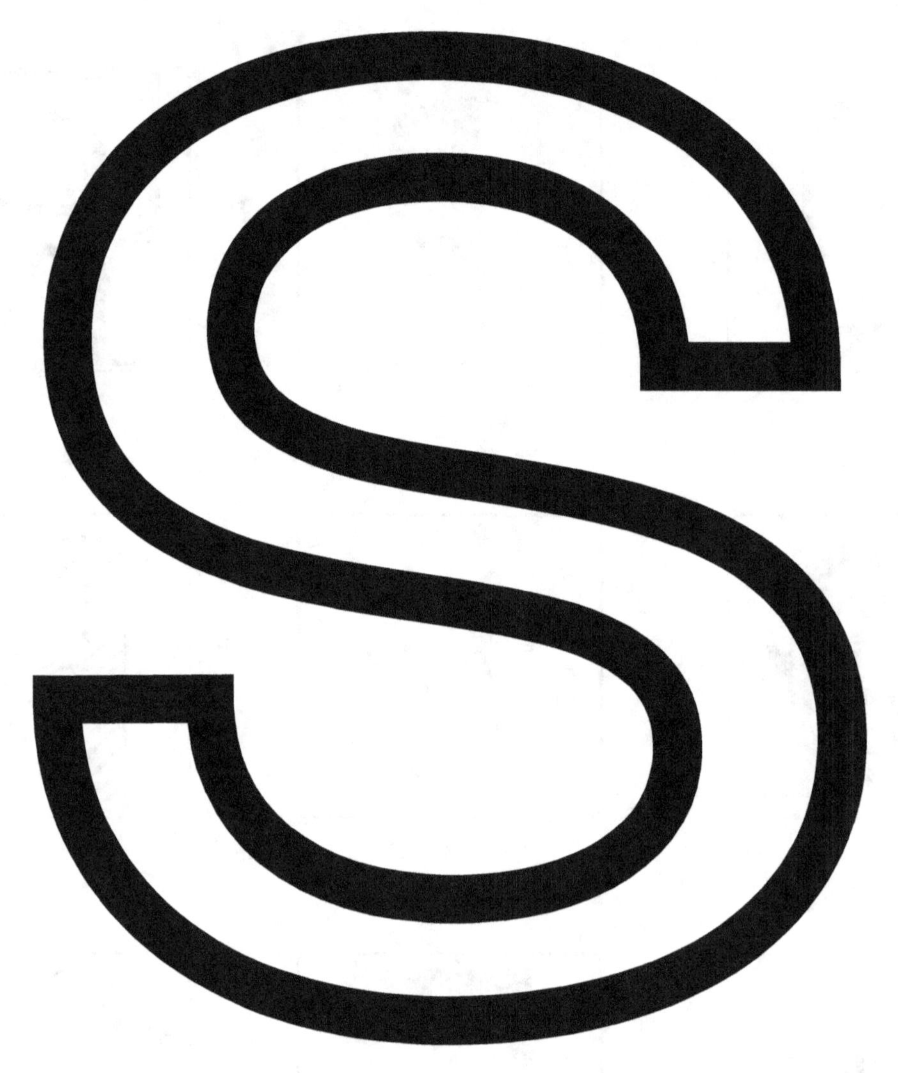

S

Color only the squares with letter S

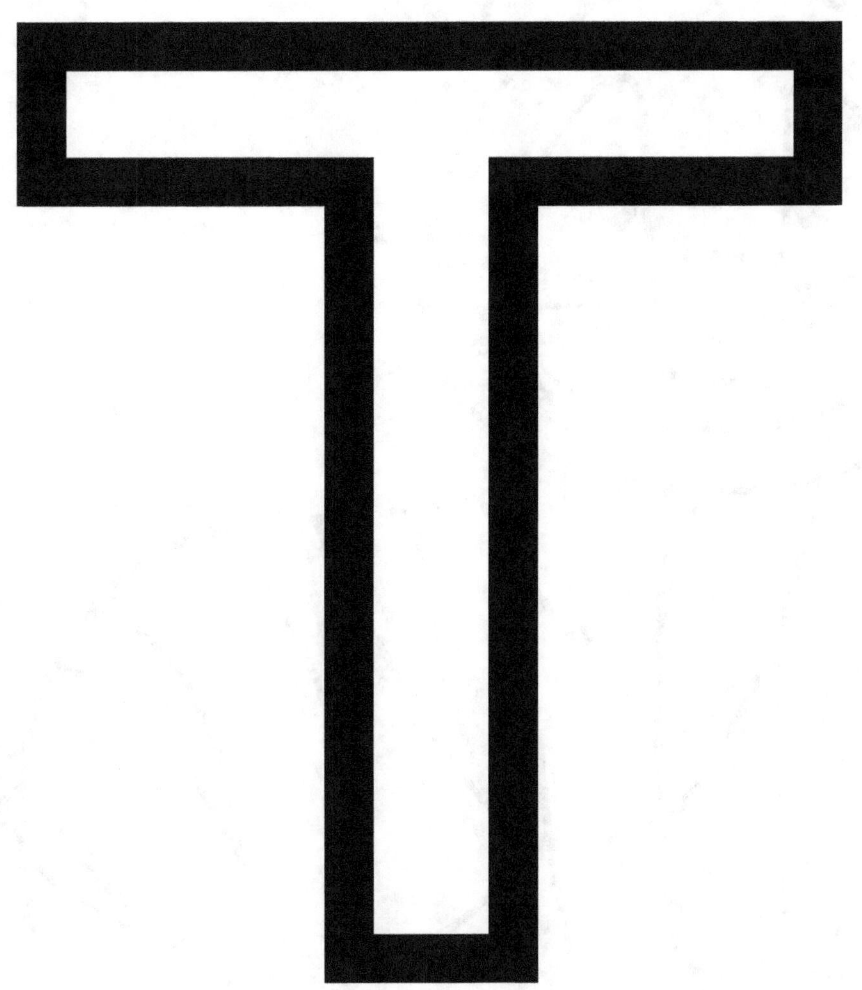

T

Color only the squares with letter T

U

U

Color only the squares with letter U

Color only the squares with letter V

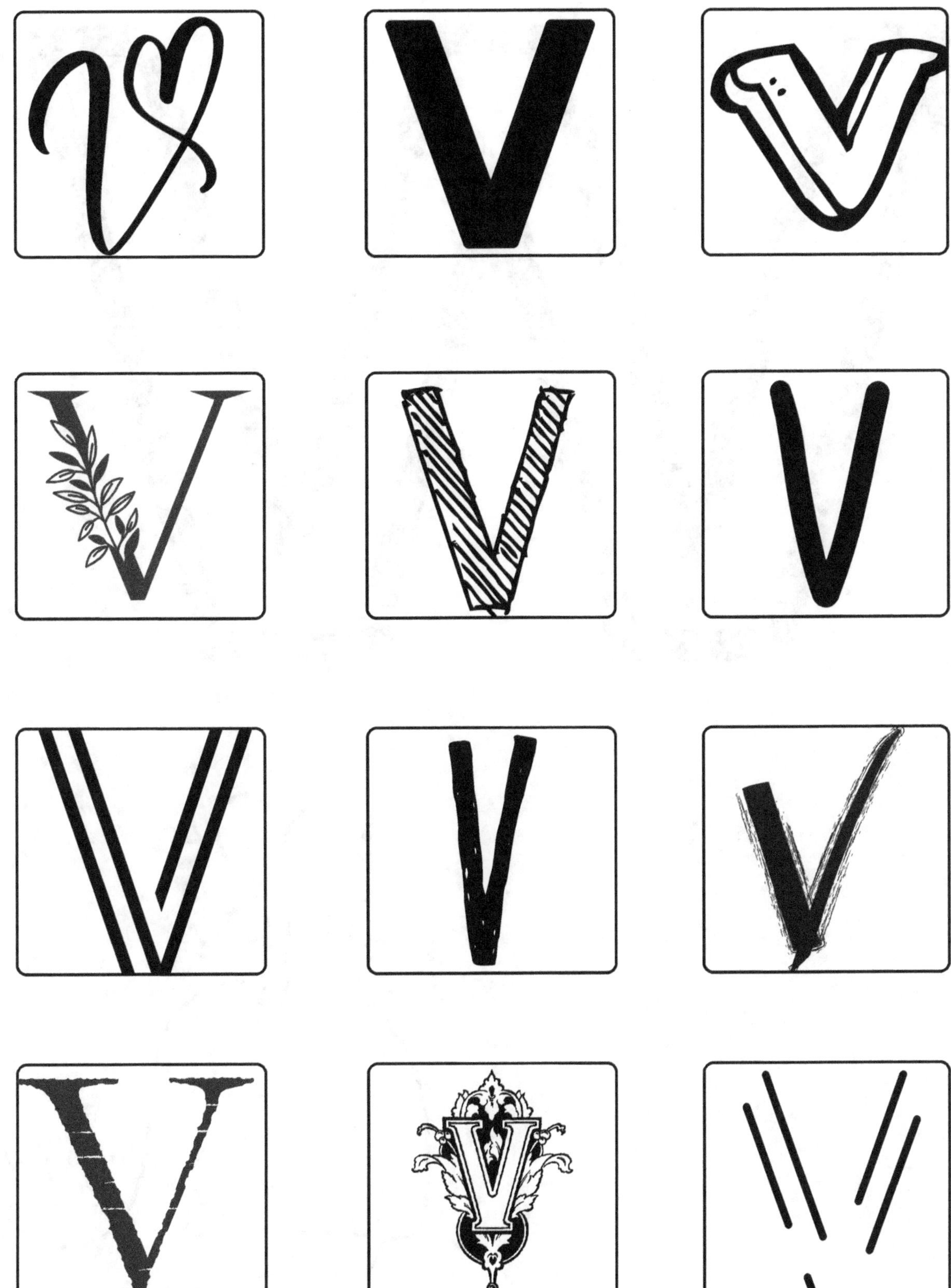

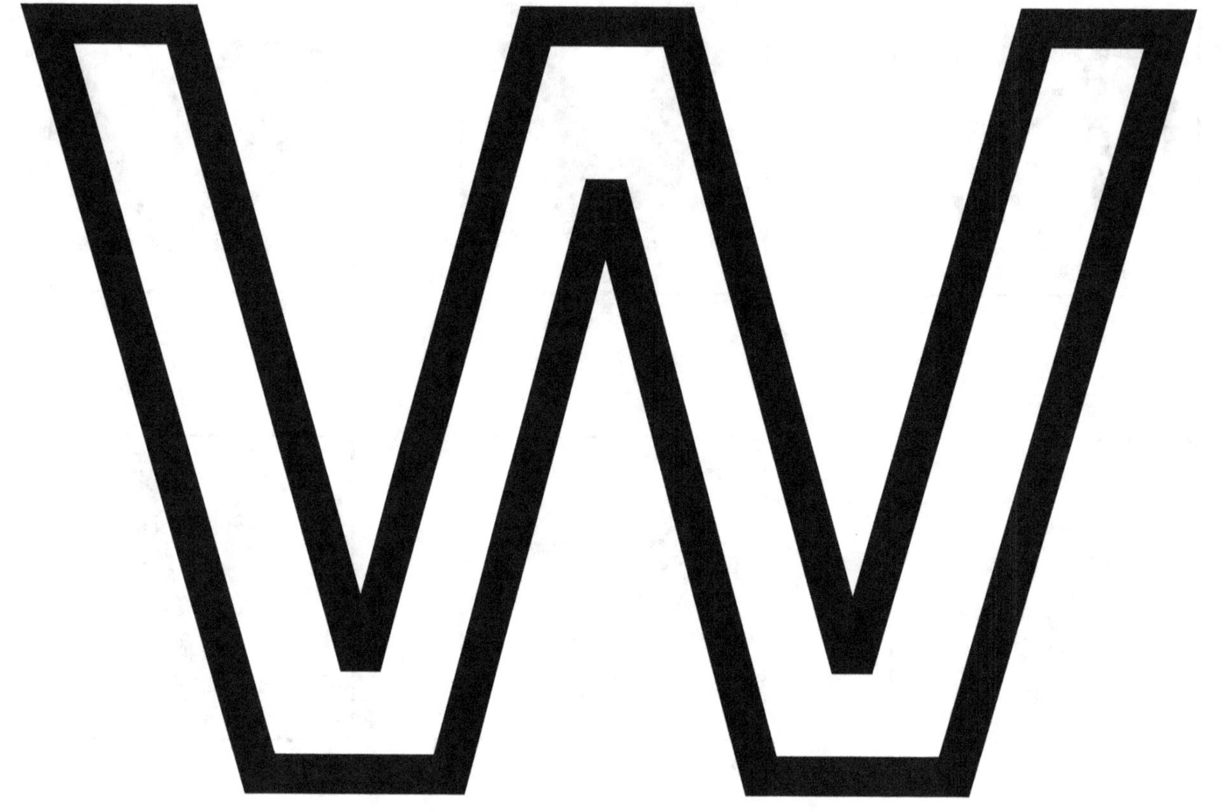

W

Color only the squares with letter W

 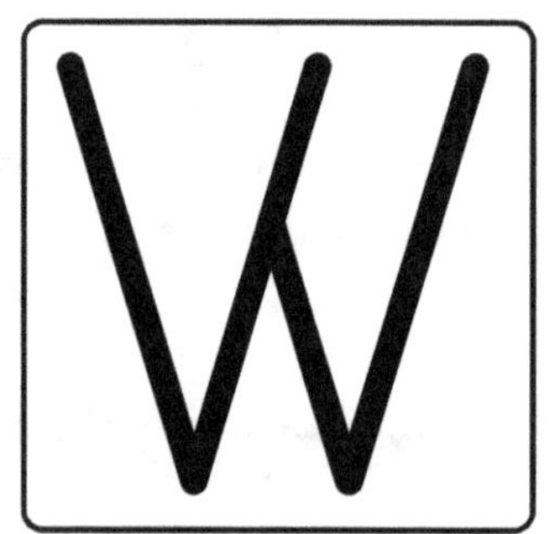 

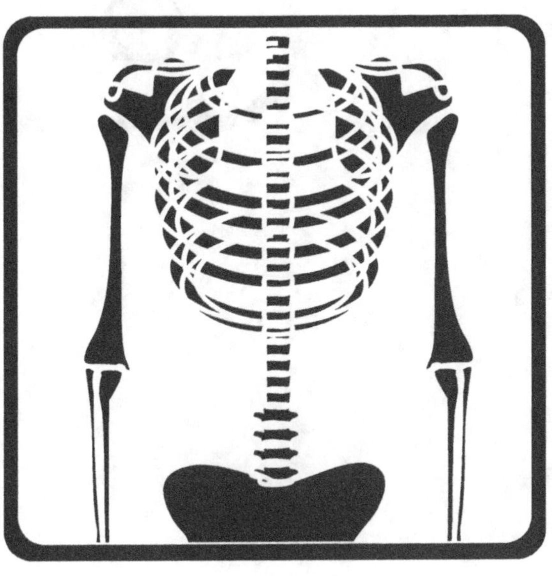

Color only the squares with letter X

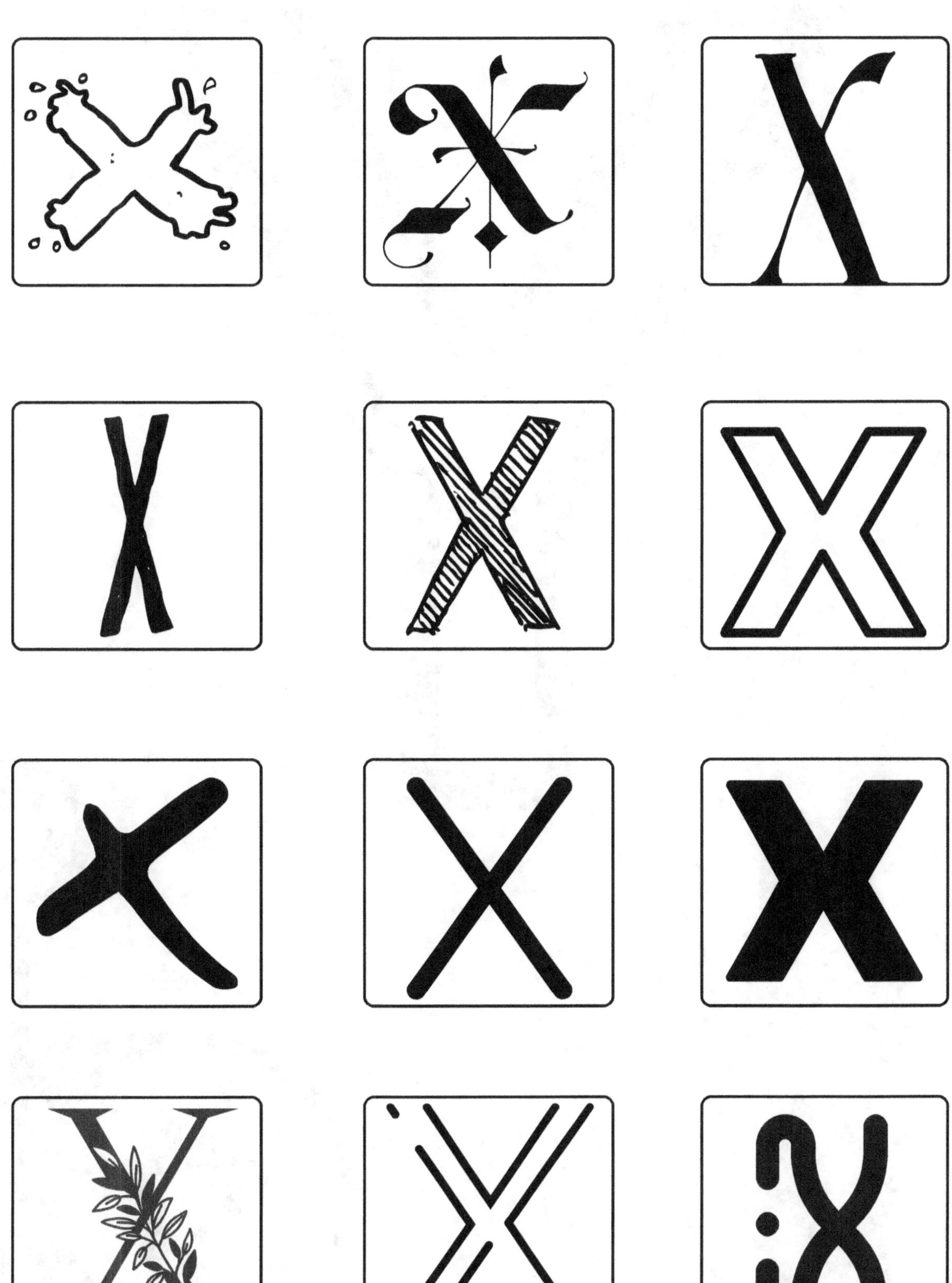

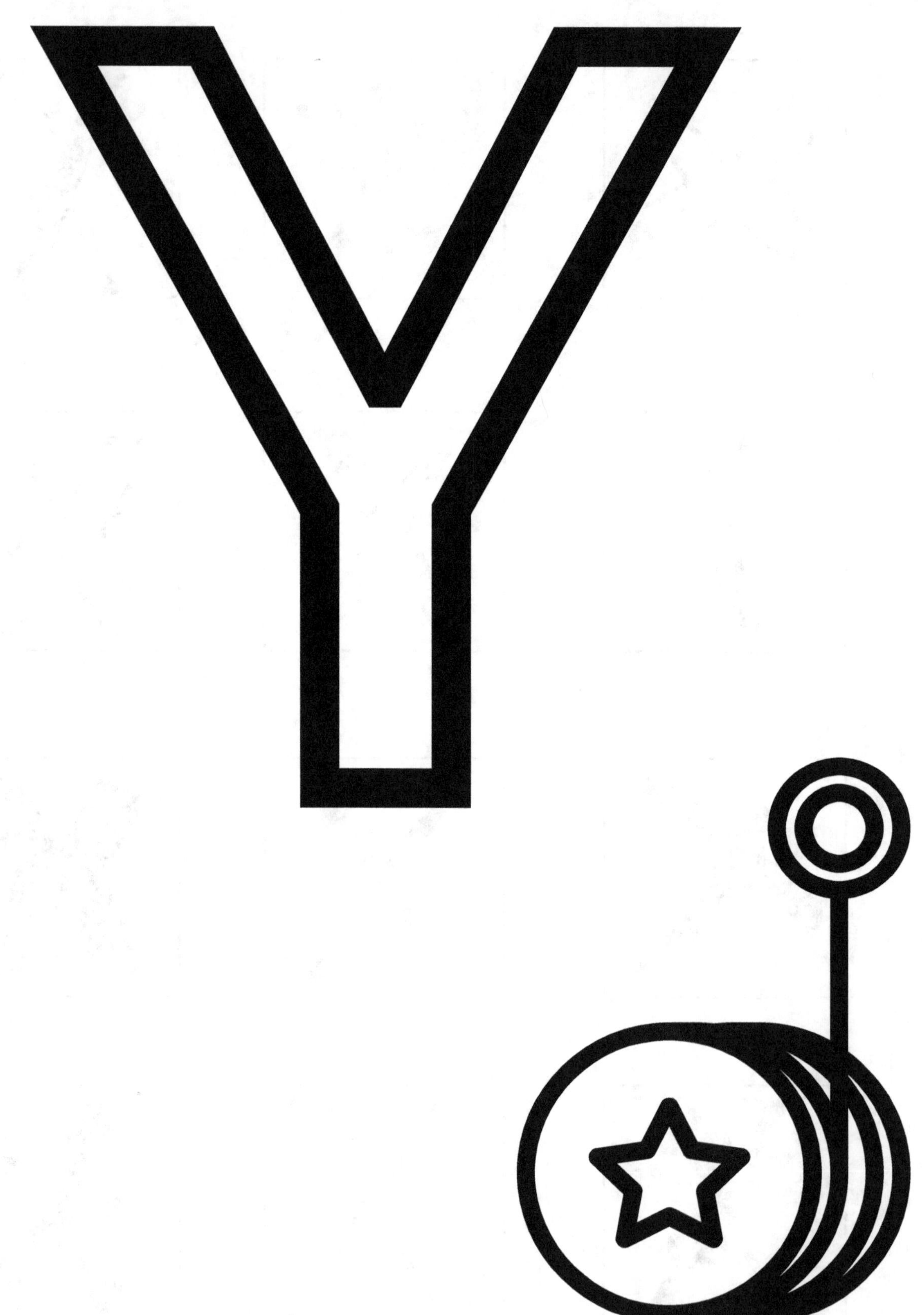

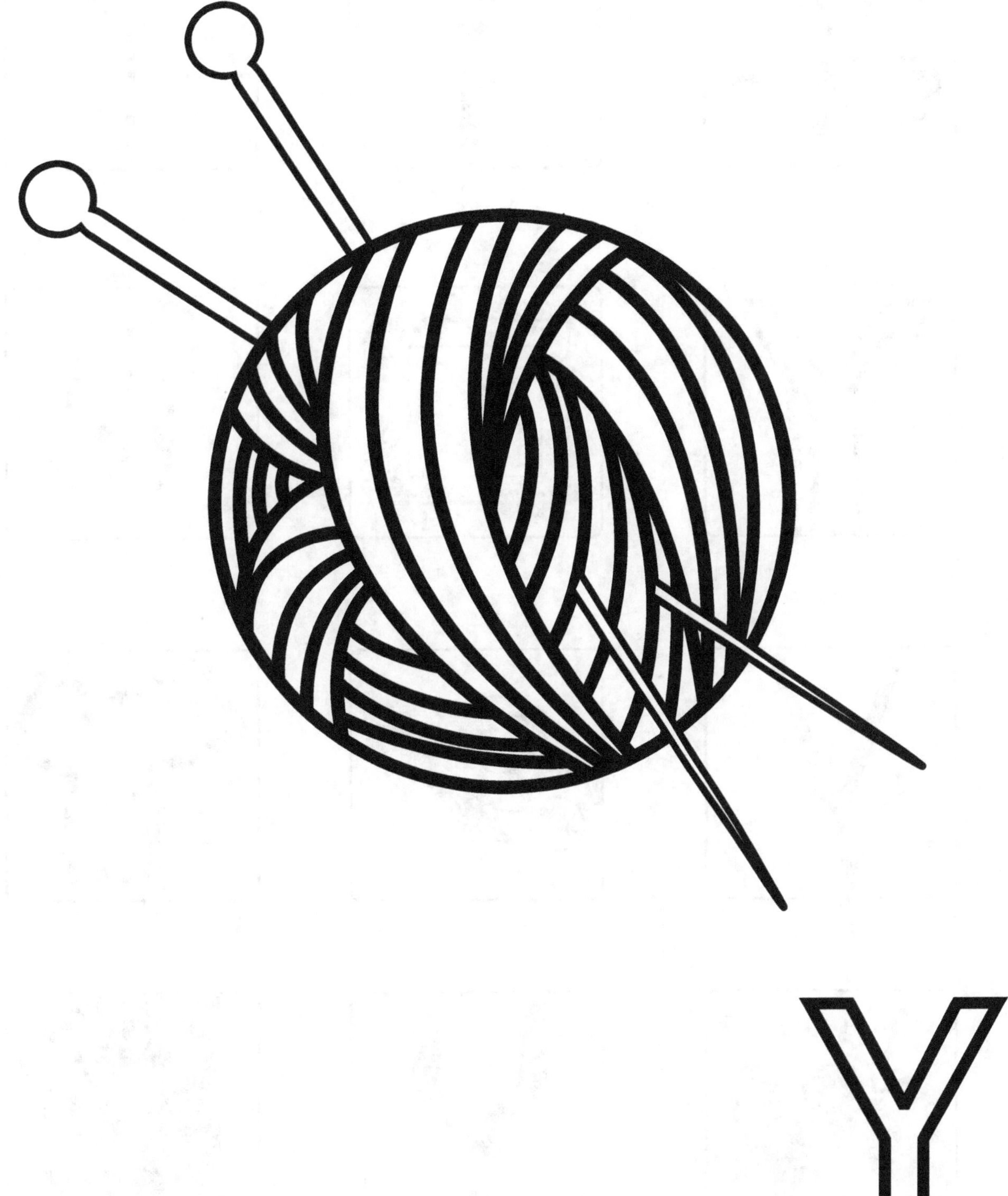

Y

Color only the squares with letter Y

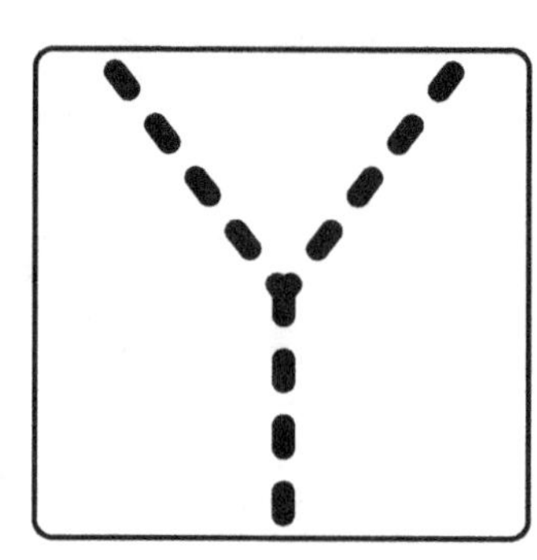

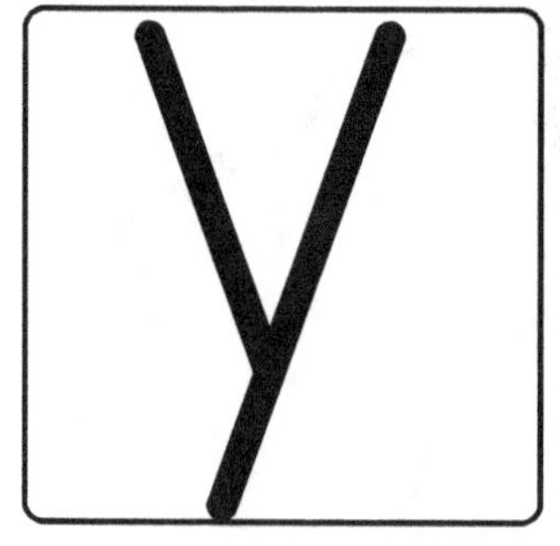

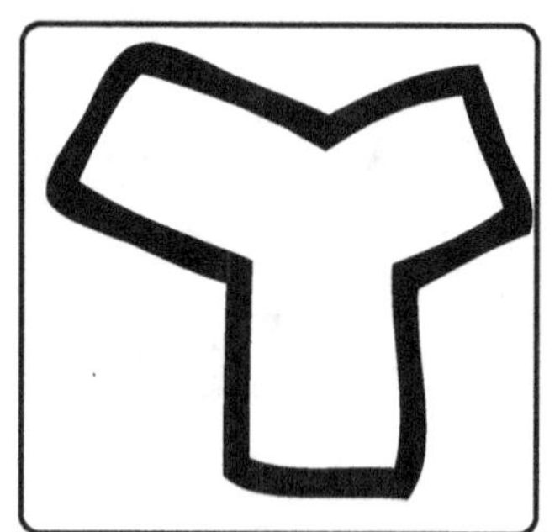
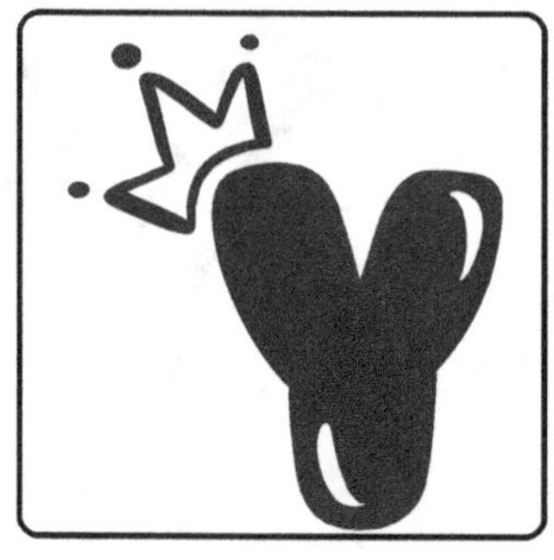

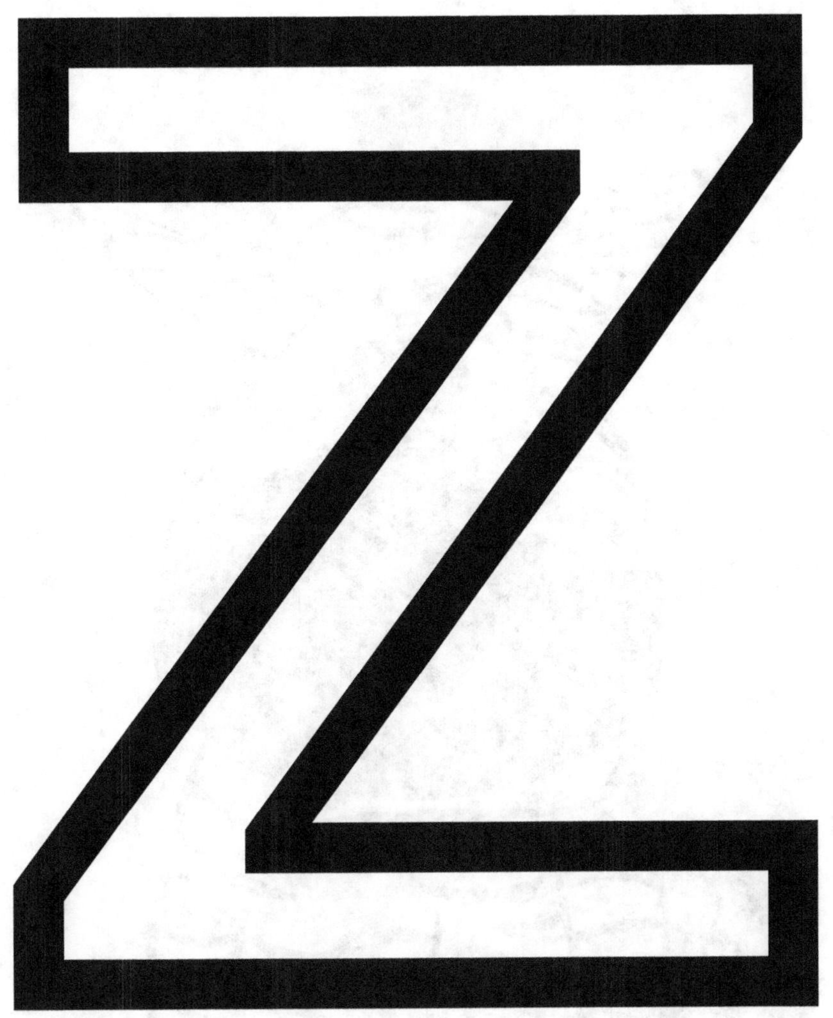

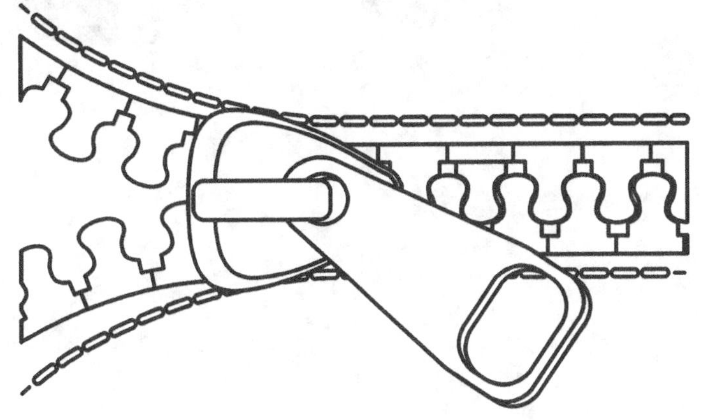

Z

Color only the squares with letter Z

Numbers

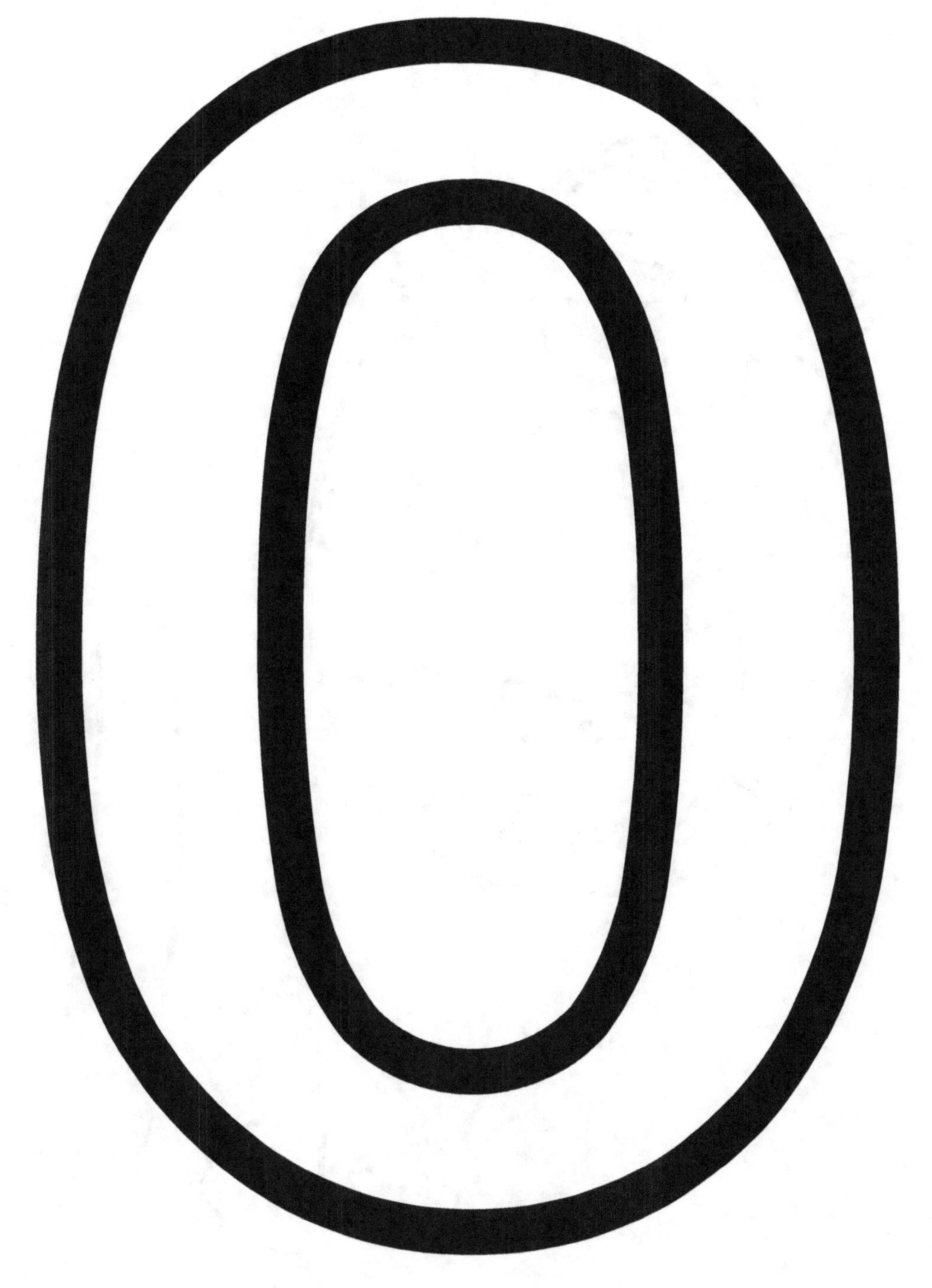

Zero

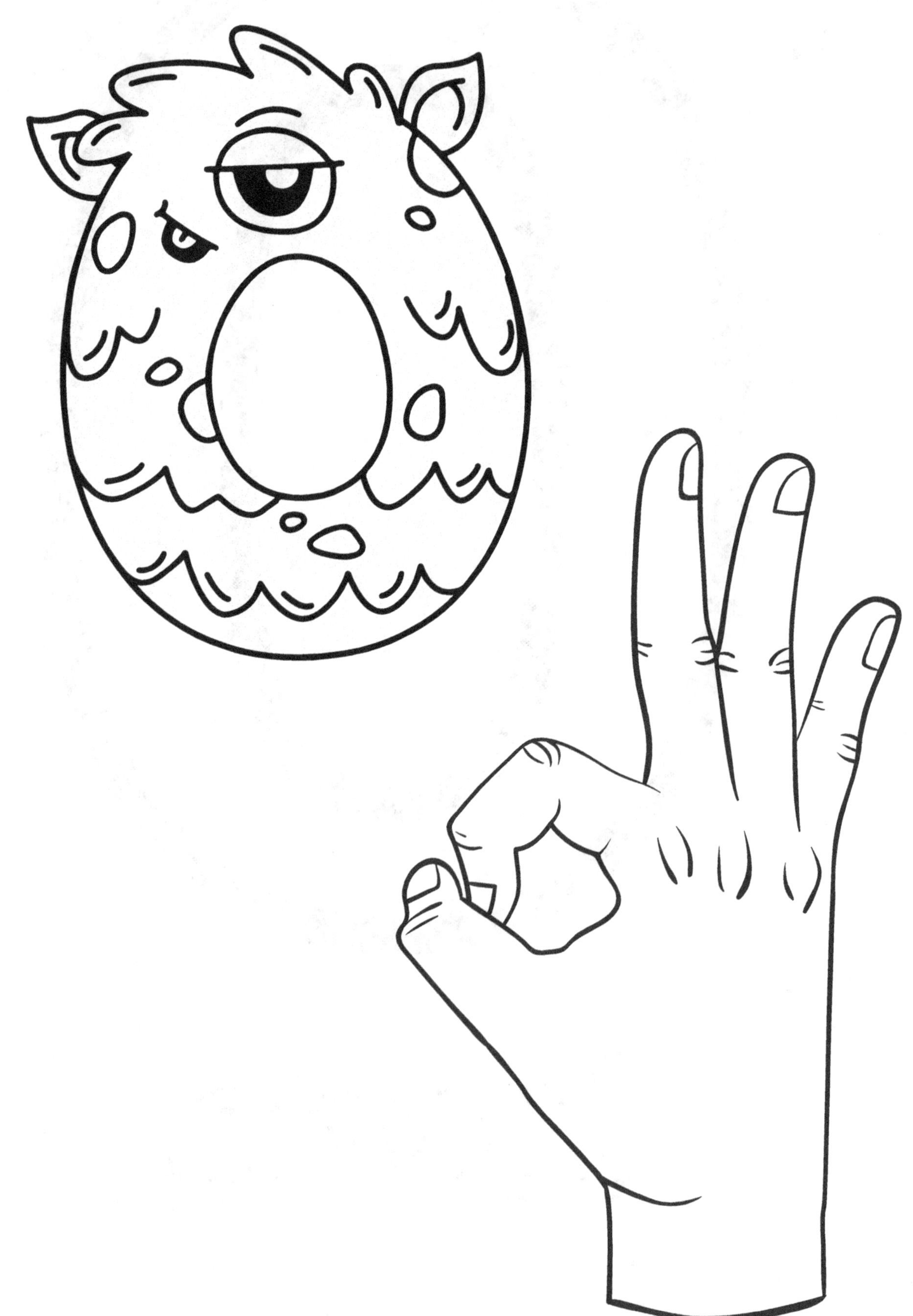

Color the trees that have 0 apples.

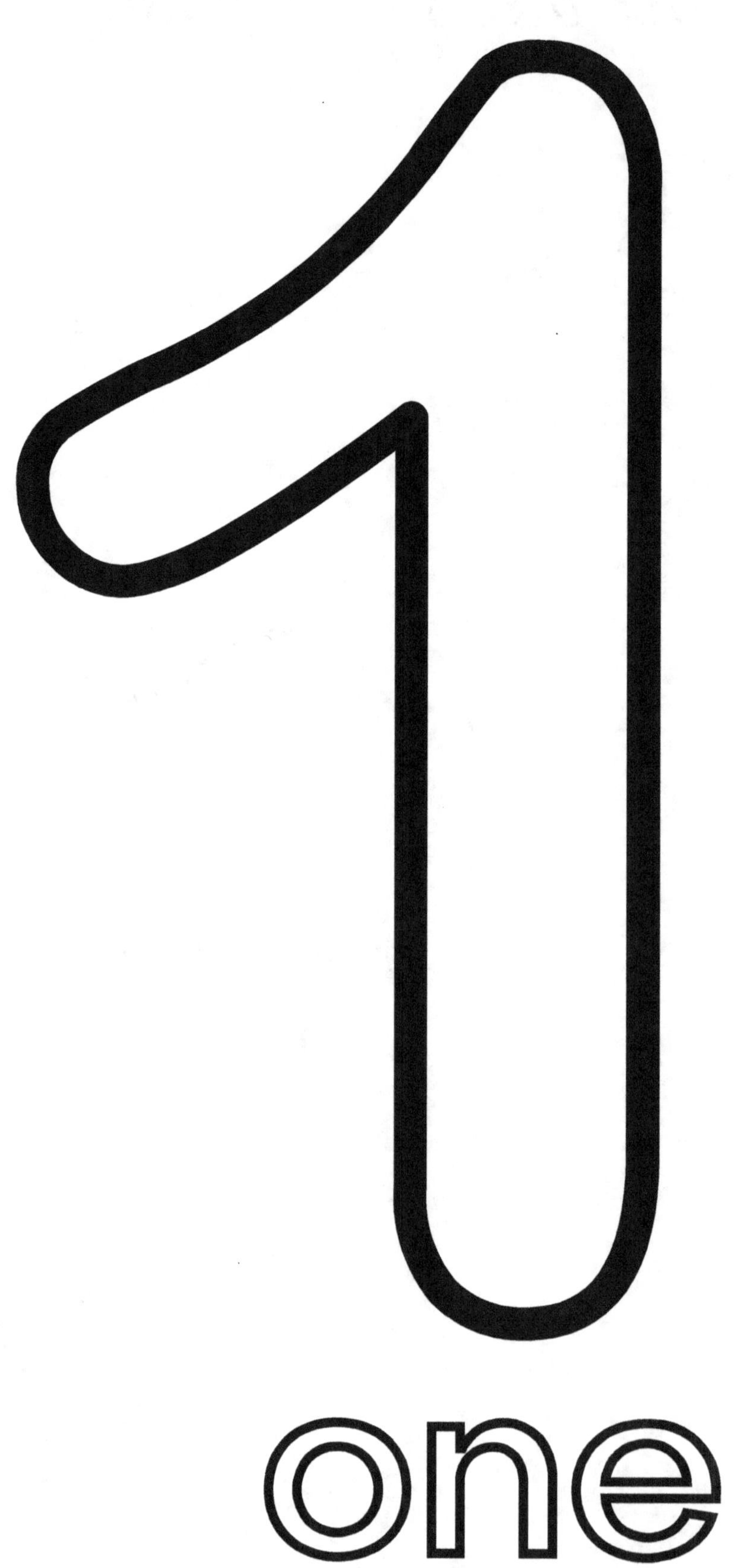

one

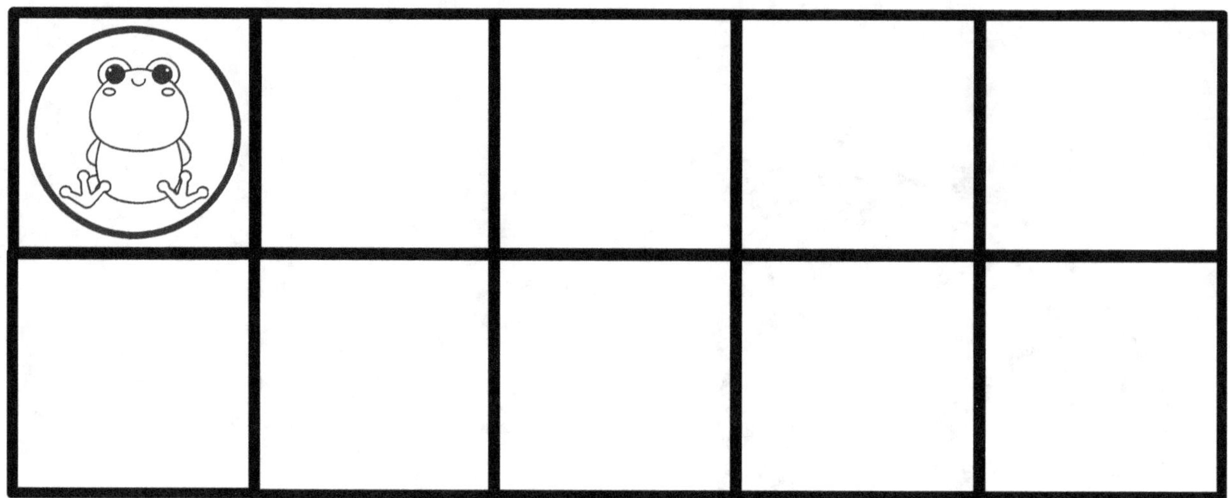

two

three

four

5
five

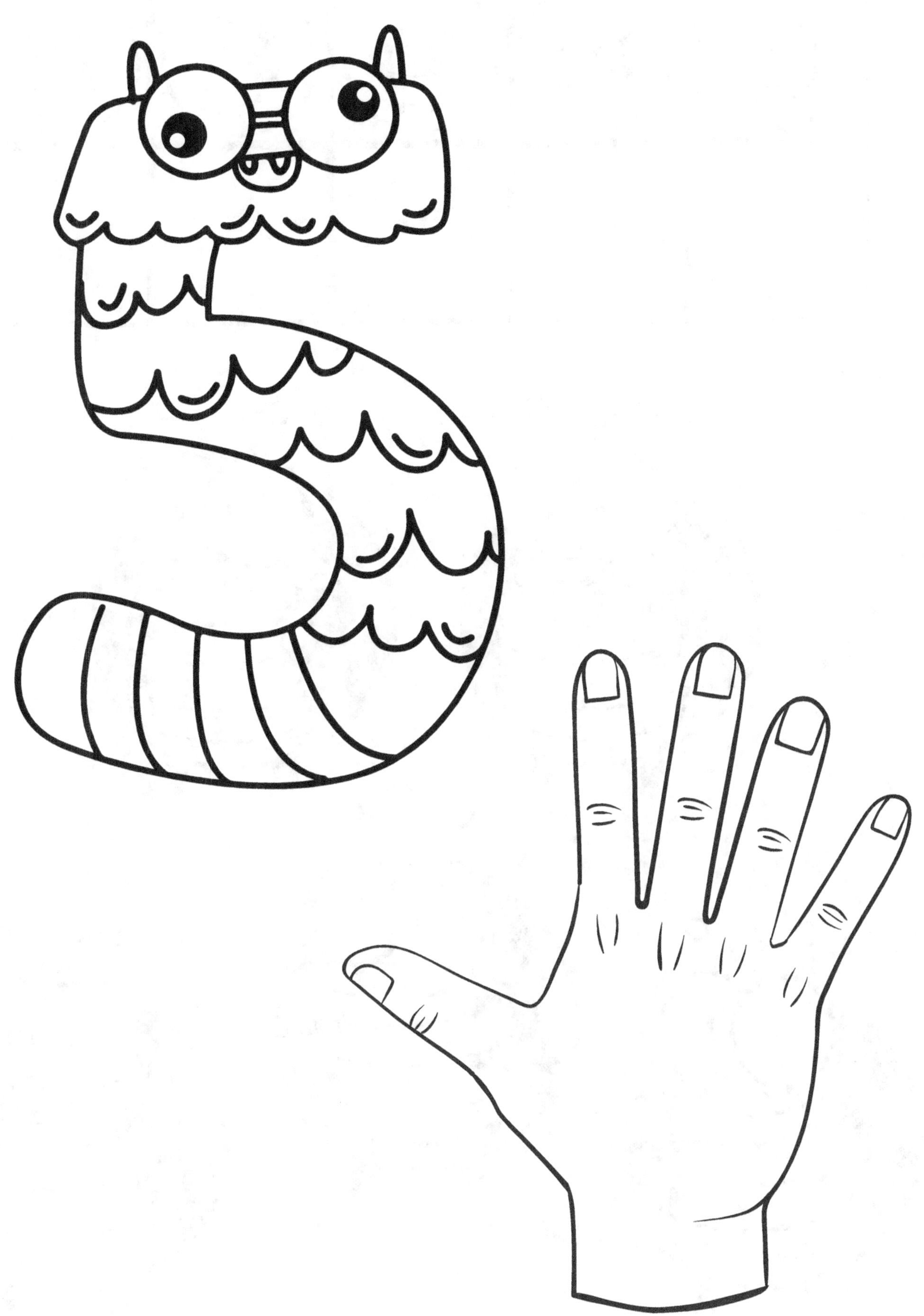

six

seven

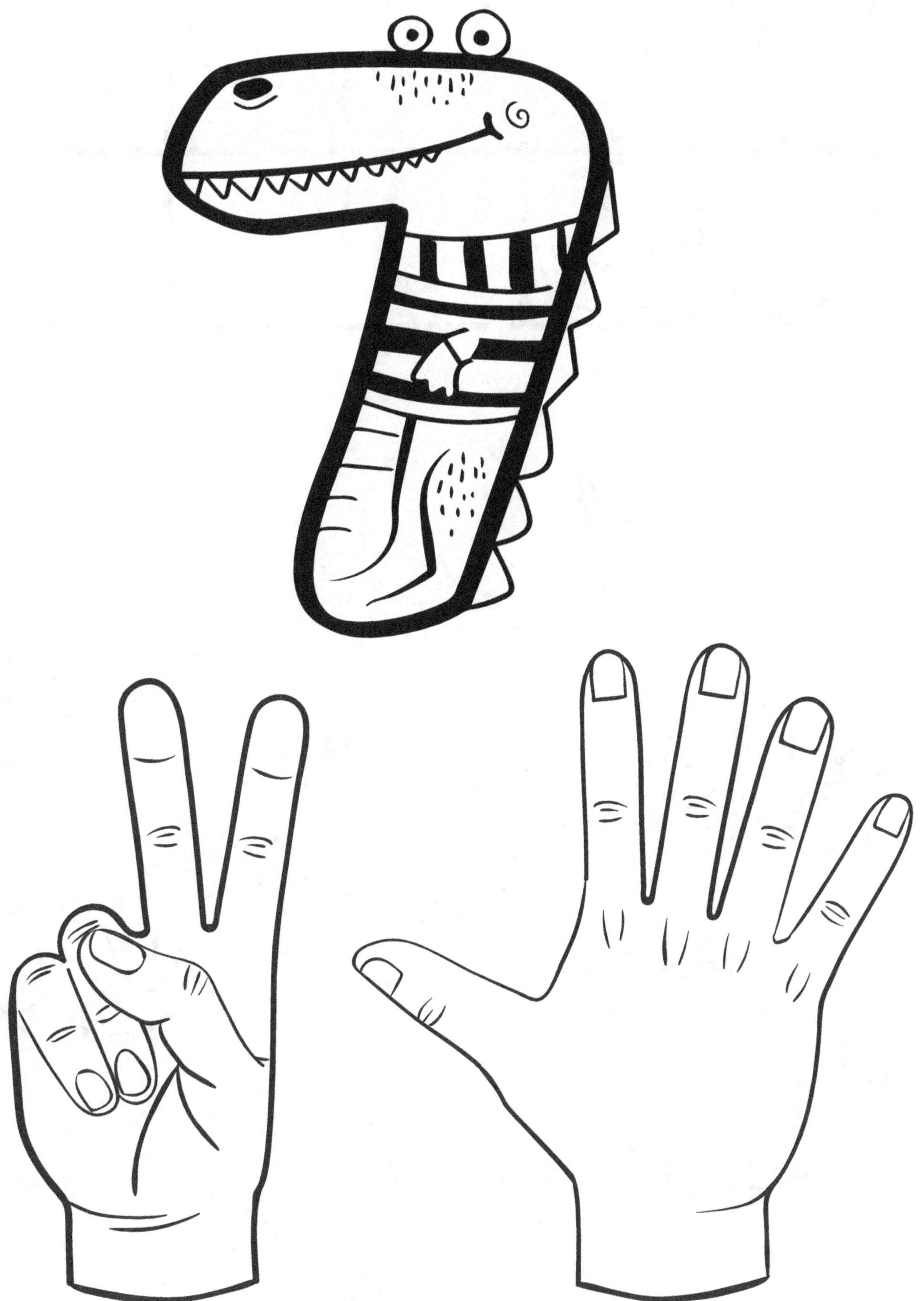

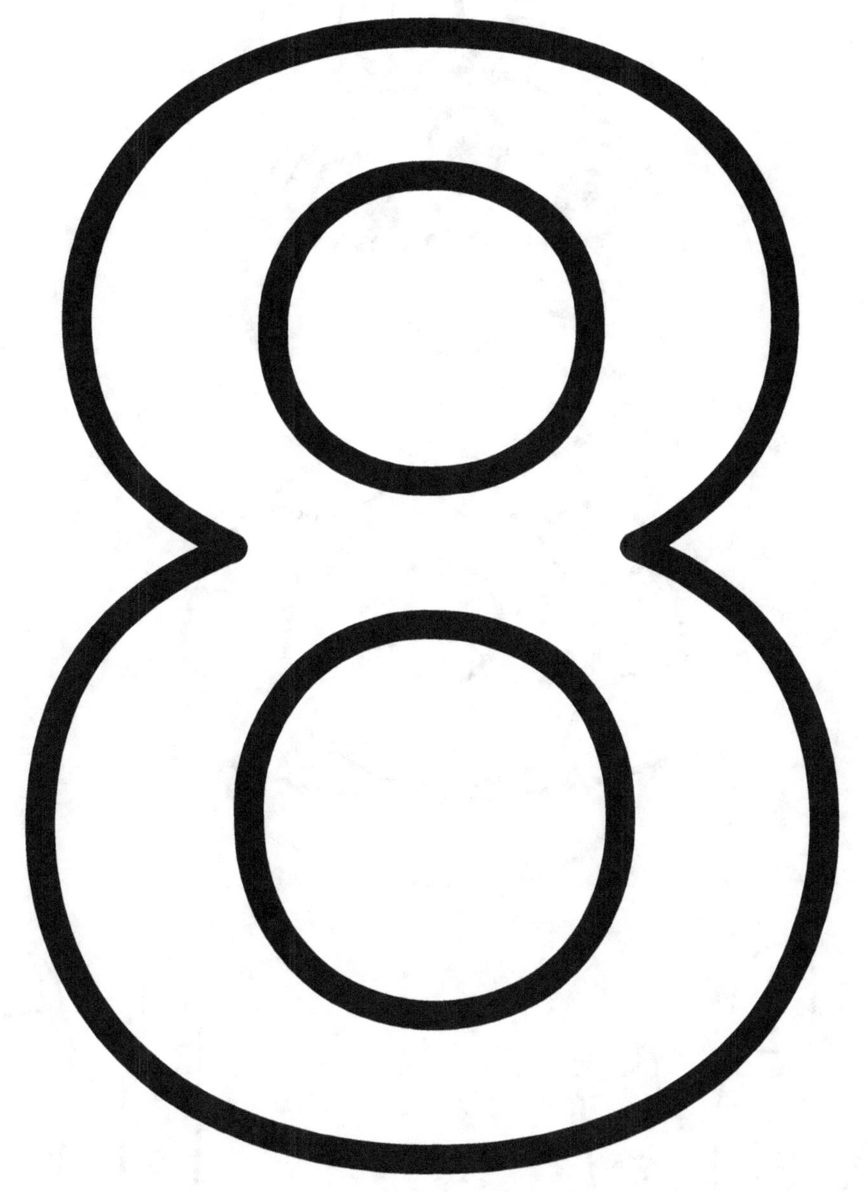

eight

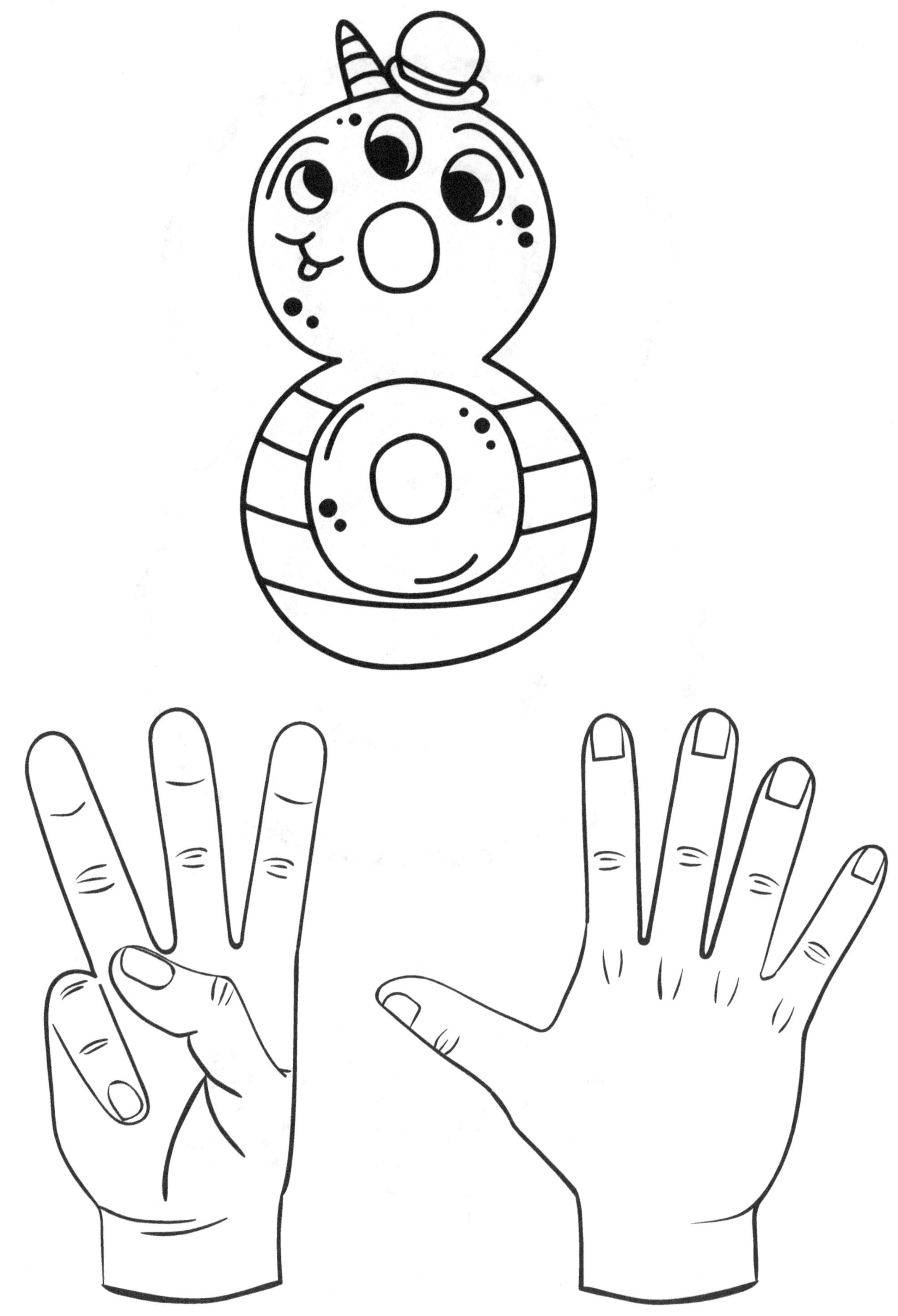

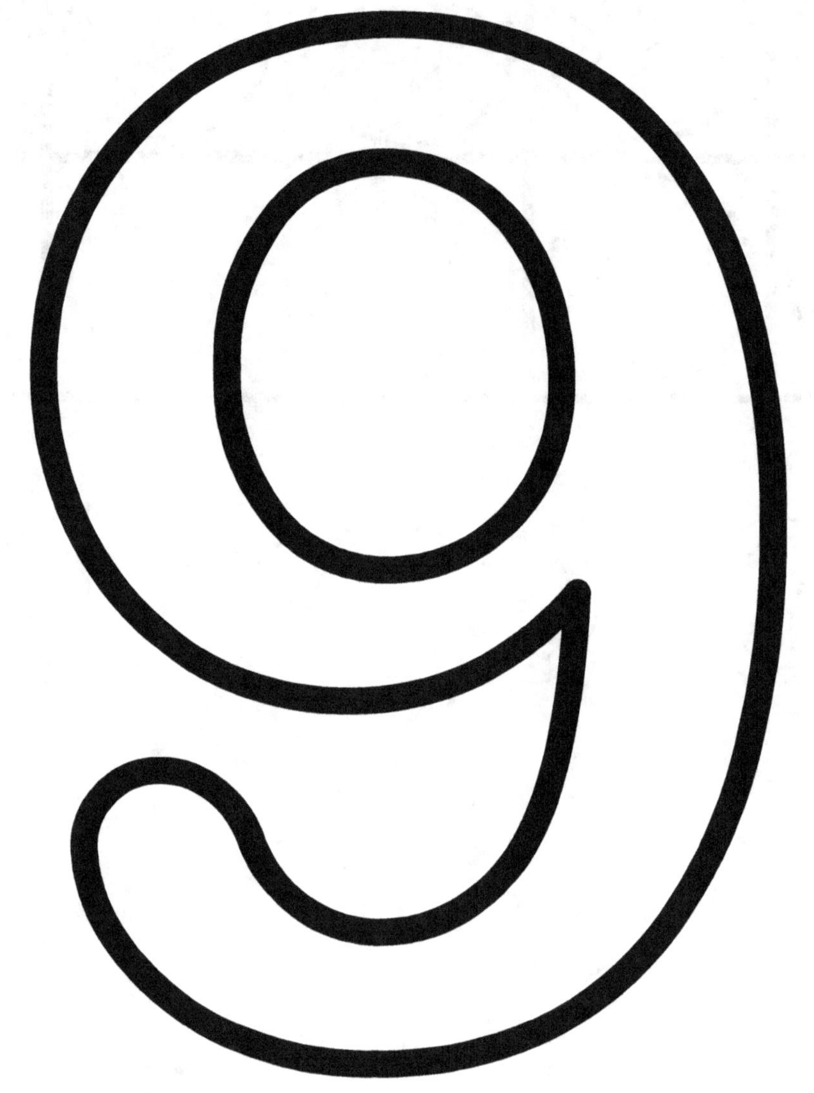

nine

10

ten

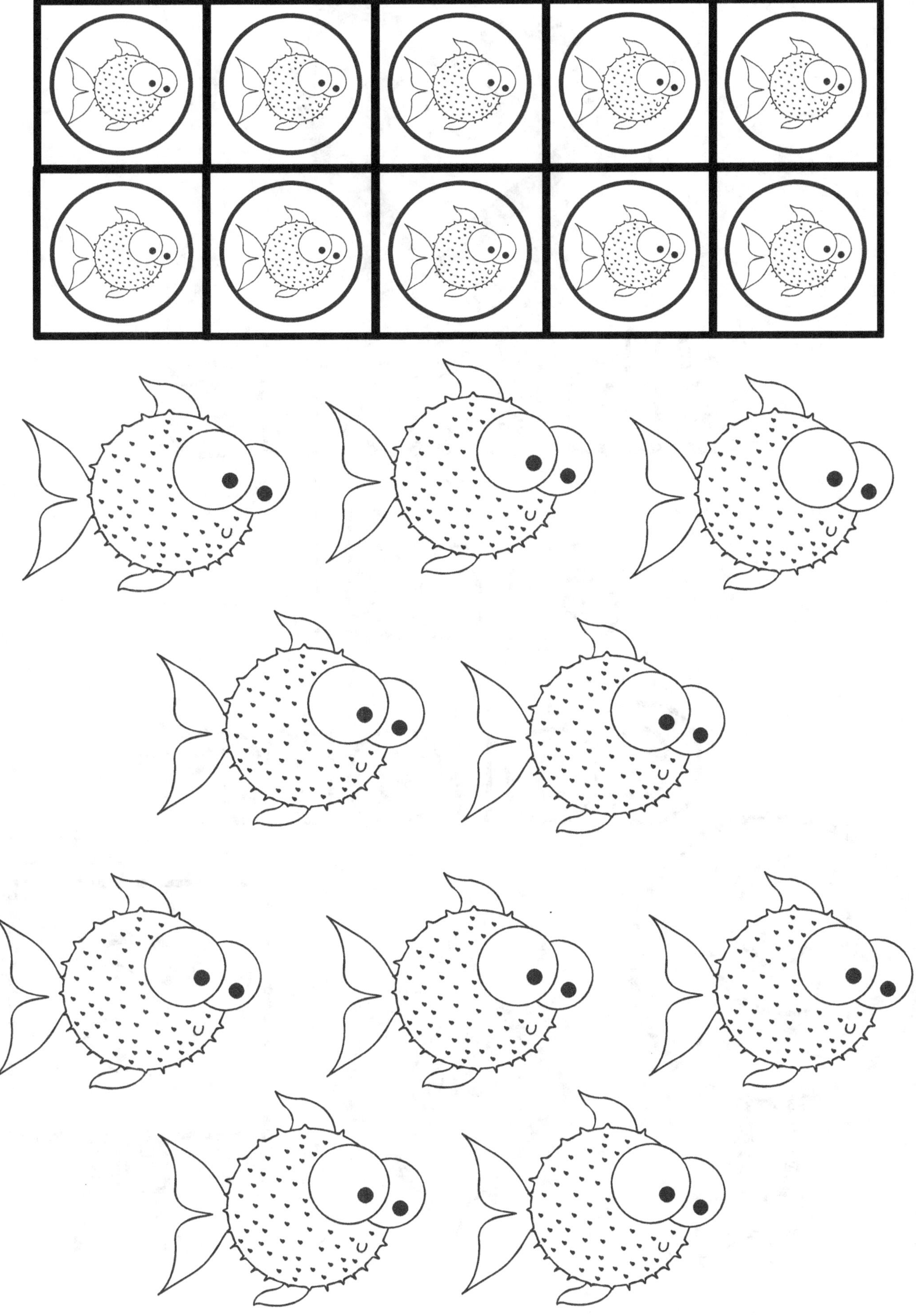

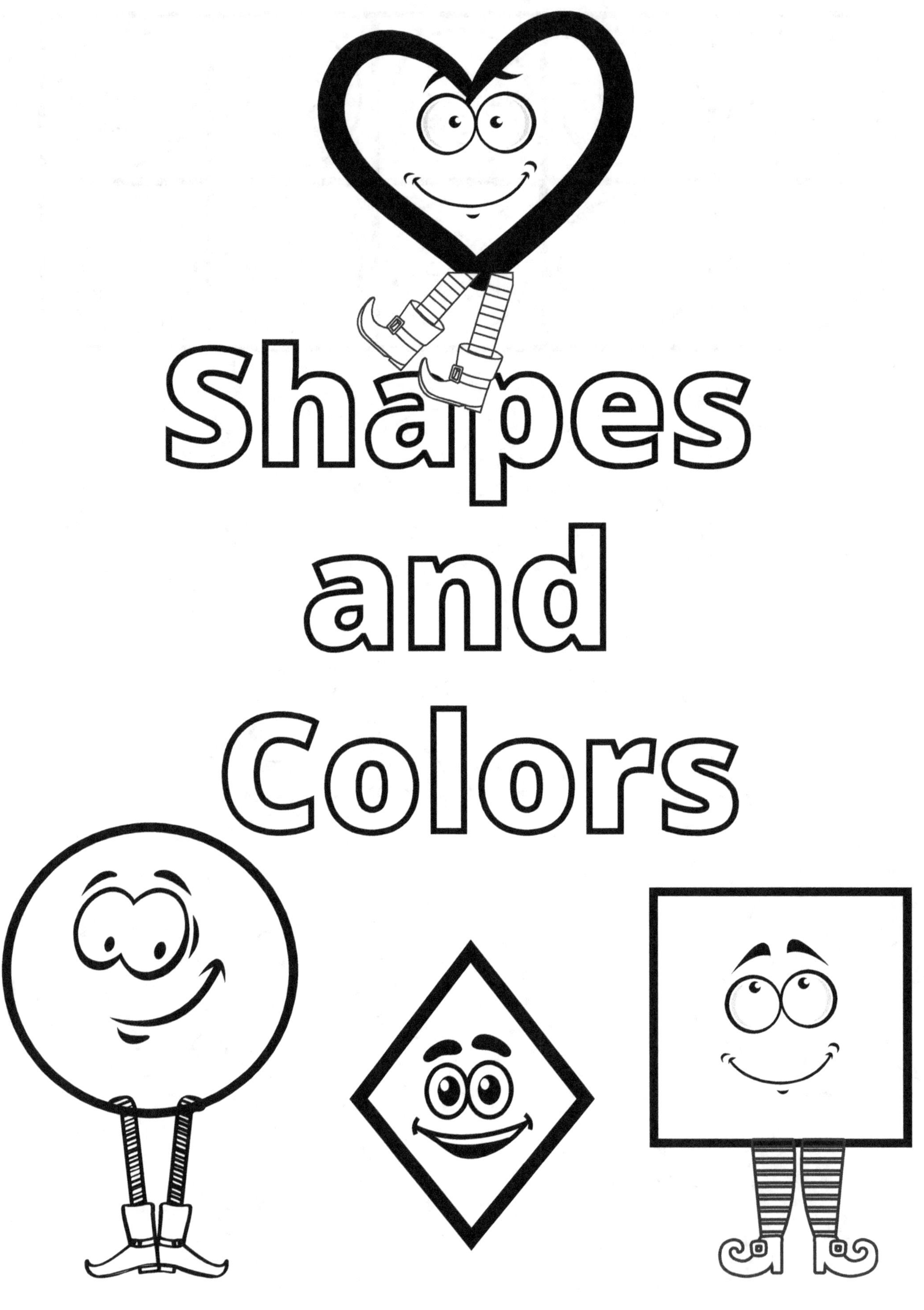

Shapes
and
Colors

Red

Orange

Yellow

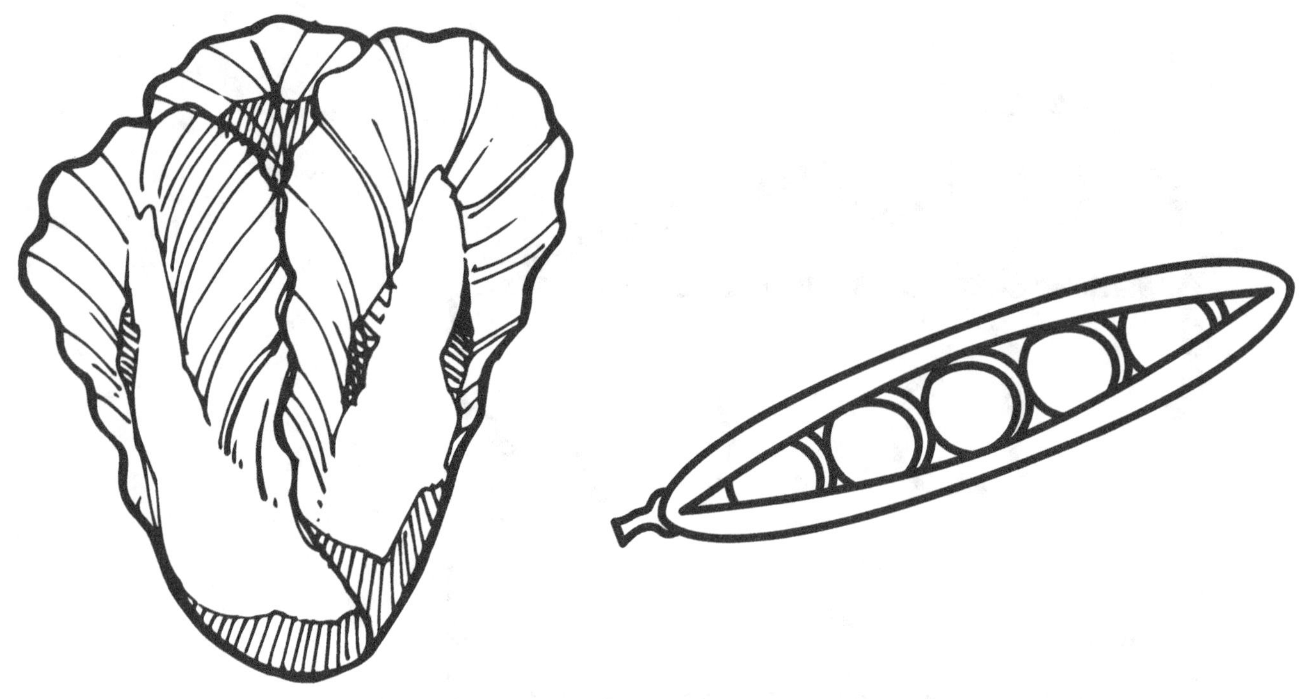

Green

Blue

Purple

Circle

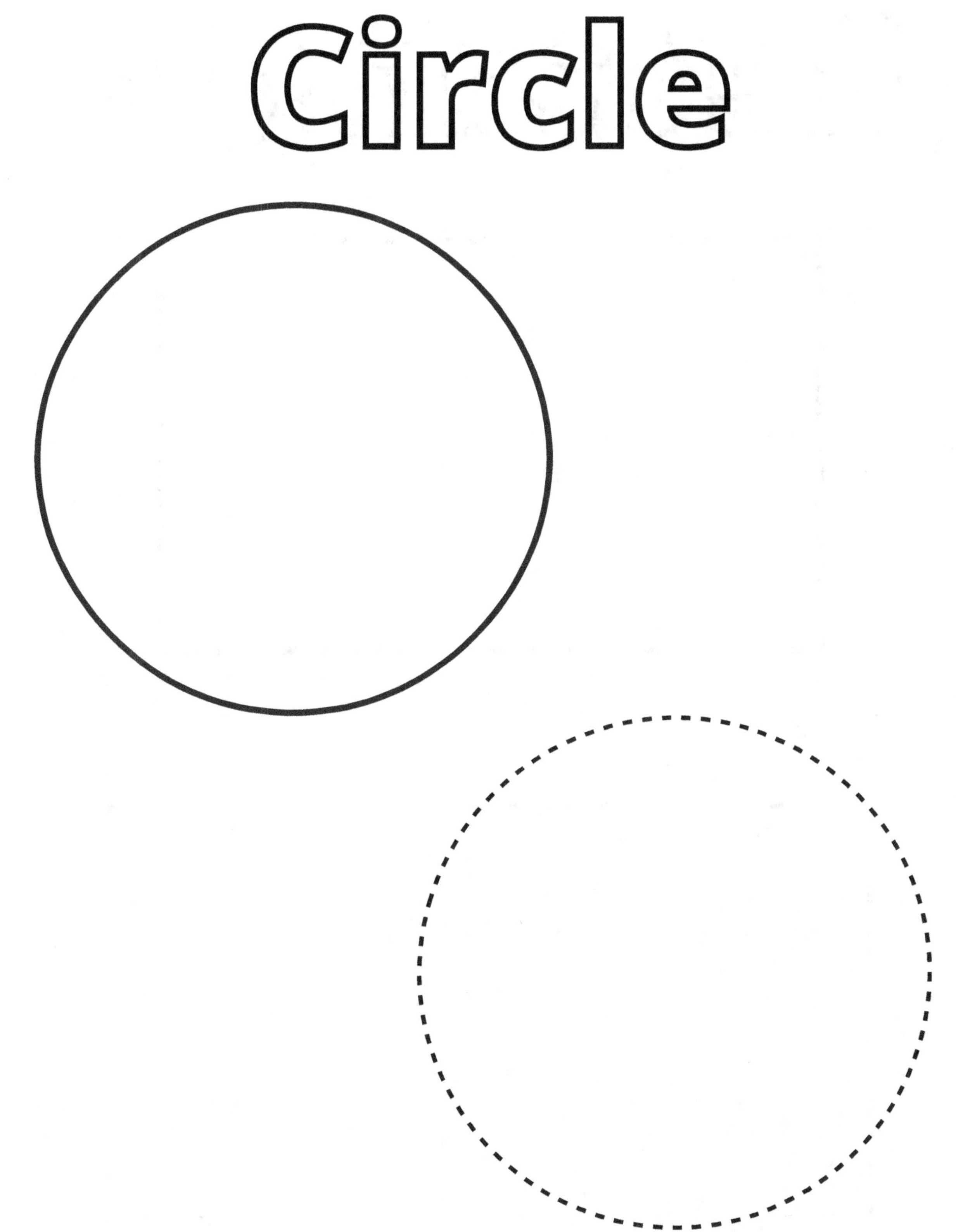

A circle is round. Color the first circle, trace the second circle and draw a face inside.

Rectangle

A rectangle has 4 sides. Two sides are long, two sides are short. Color the first rectangle, trace and draw a picture inside the second rectangle.

Square

A square has 4 equal sides. Color the first square, trace and draw a house using the second square.

Triangle

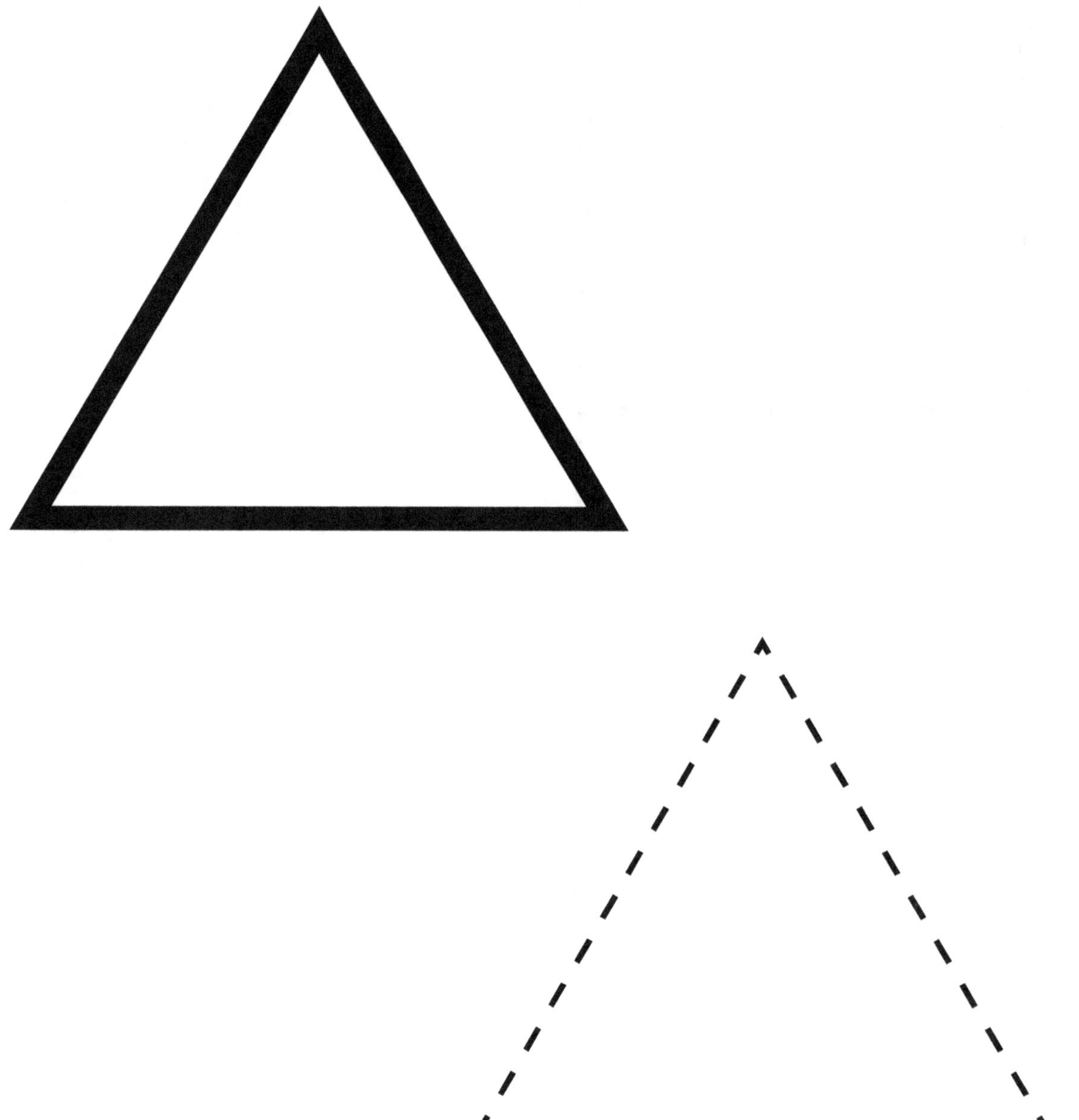

A triangle has three sides. Color the first triangle, trace and draw a pizza slice using the second square.

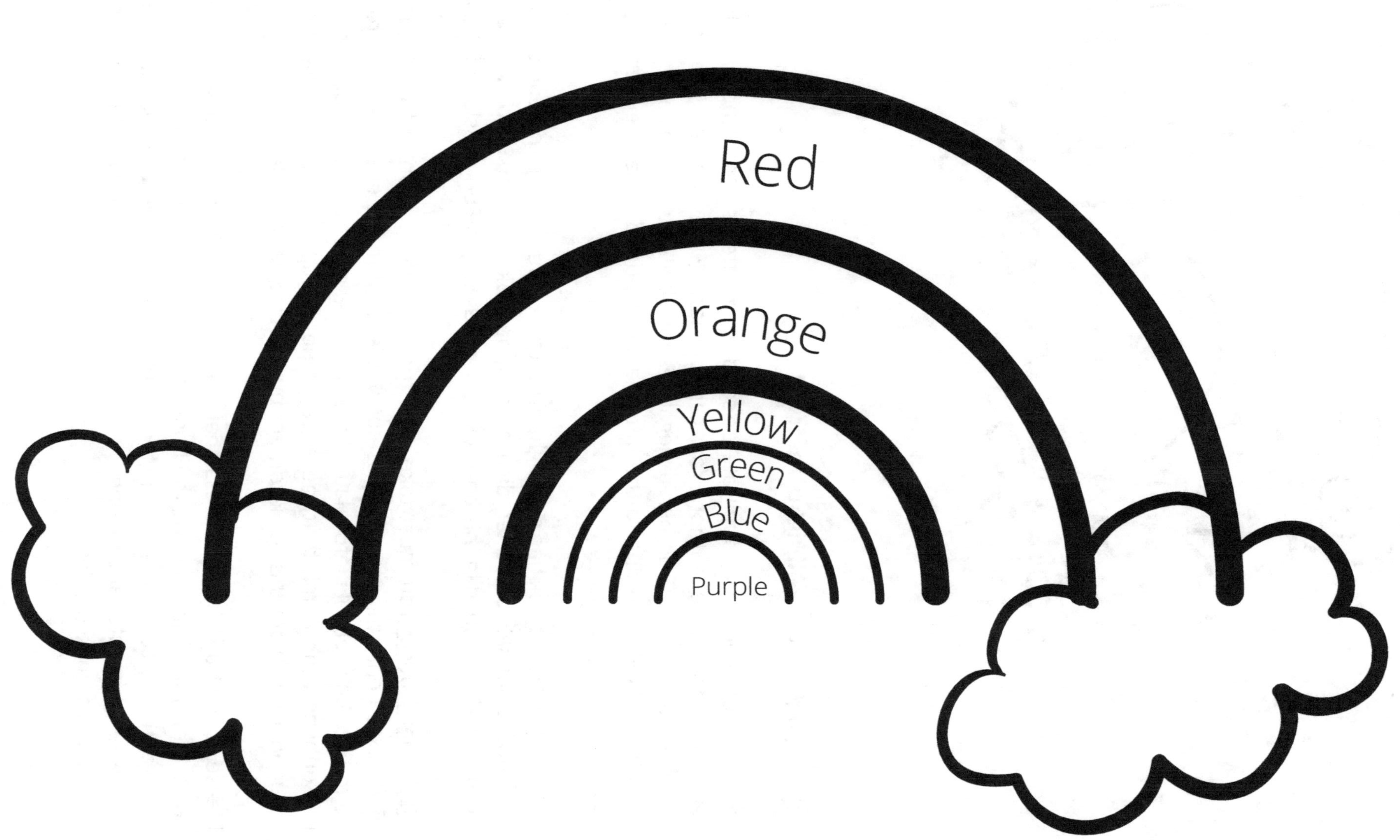

Red
Orange
Yellow
Green
Blue
Purple

You did a fabulous job!

Thank you.

We hope you enjoyed our book.

As a small family company, your feedback is very important to us.

Please let us know how you like our book at:

helen.m.anvil@gmail.com

/helen.anvil

/helen.anvil

Great Job!
AWARD
Name
Finished his/her
123s and ABCs
You're # 1